General Editor:
Patrick McNeill

KU-255-812

SOCIETY
NOW

Work, Unemployment, and Leisure

Other books in the **Society Now** series

Rosemary Deem

WORK, UNEMPLOYMENT, and LEISURE

R

Routledge · London

First published in 1988 by
Routledge
11 New Fetter Lane,
London EC4P 4EE

© 1988 Rosemary Deem

Set by Hope Services, Abingdon
Printed in Great Britain by
The Guernsey Press
Channel Islands

*British Library Cataloguing
in Publication Data*
Deem, Rosemary, 1949–
Work and leisure.—(Society now).
1. Great Britain. Leisure. Work &
leisure.
Social aspects
I. Title   II. Series
306′.36

ISBN 0 415 00860 3

Contents

Acknowledgments

I should like to thank Pat McNeill for encouraging me to write this book. My thoughts on work and leisure have particularly been shaped by being a part of the Open University course team which produced DE325 Work and Society in 1985 and I am grateful to the members of that team for their stimulating discussions. Thanks are also due to Kevin Brehony, Maureen Clark, and Spencer Phelan, whose own experiences of teaching A Level sociology have been enormously helpful to me.

1

Introducing work and leisure

The terms work and leisure are likely to be extremely familiar ones to you, since they are in common use in our everyday lives. What this book hopes to do is to take you beyond your own experiences of these two phenomena into a sociological exploration of the meanings, structures, and patterns of work in contemporary societies, with a particular focus on the United Kingdom. It will look at the relationship between working and being involved in leisure, different varieties of work including employment in the formal economy, casual work, and forms of unpaid work, the effects of unemployment, and varieties of leisure. There will also, in the final chapter, be a discussion about change in work and leisure. In so doing there will be a particular focus on empirical studies, although theoretical perspectives will not be forgotten altogether. If however you are wanting very basic information about sociological perspectives and the sociology of work, you would be well advised to precede your reading of this book with a prior reading of a standard introductory textbook such as Haralambros (1985), because lack of space will prevent this book from dwelling on topics like bureaucracy, industrial conflict, and occupational associations, amongst others. However, what the book will do is to relate the study of work and leisure to a considerable number of other areas including class stratification and other social divisions, culture, the state, the family, and education.

Berger (1963) has said that 'the first wisdom of sociology is this – things are seldom what they seem' and this is particularly true of work and leisure. Firstly we tend to assume that things are today much as they have always been; that our notions of work and leisure are timeless, when historically it is easy to show that for example such taken for granted things as paid holidays are a very recent development. Secondly, we also tend to assume that the experiences of others are similar to our own; that if our idea of leisure is watching TV or going to the pub then so is everyone else's. But gender, class, and age, for example, have a powerful effect on what leisure we have, what we do with it, and how much we value it. The same is also true of work – there are many different experiences and meanings, so that a happy factory worker, an unhappy secretary, an unemployed woman, and a 70-year-old retired man will relate to and perceive paid and unpaid work in different ways. Nevertheless our own ideas about work and leisure provide a valuable jumping-off point; we are after all just as much a social product as the next person and our ideas are seldom unique. So let's spend just a little time thinking about how leisure and work might be defined.

Activity

Write down in not more than two sentences what the terms work and leisure mean to you. Then get someone else, preferably someone unlike yourself, to tell you what they understand by these terms (e.g. if you are female ask a male, if you are a teenager ask an adult) and compare the two sets of definitions.

You may well have defined work and leisure as two things which are opposite to each other; work is something we are obliged to do, like writing an essay, sitting an exam, or earning a living, whilst leisure is something which we choose to do and find enjoyable (such as swimming, listening to music, playing football, going out for a meal) when we are not working. The other person you asked may have had similar ideas to yourself; but it's possible for example that if you asked a busy housewife what leisure was, she'd say she didn't have any or that she relaxed by watching TV whilst ironing and supervising her children. If you asked a professional worker, say a residential social worker, they might say that their work and leisure blend into one and they can't distinguish them – both are enjoyable. An unemployed person might say that work in the form of a job is something they'd like to do if they had the chance because it provides money and status, but that they have far too much leisure or 'time on their hands'. Defining work and leisure, then, is far from straightforward, since any definition needs to be set in its social and historical context; there's no such thing as a universal definition of either term. But it may be useful to look at a couple of definitions relevant to contemporary industrial societies.

Finnegan (1985a) suggests that the following are possible characteristics of work in contemporary Britain: a high division of labour and specialization of tasks (unlike a society where there is subsistence farming say, and everyone does everything), differentiation of the economic from other aspects of society (for example the family or religion), a relative separation of work from leisure (although as we've seen this doesn't hold for everyone), bureaucratic and impersonal organization of most work, and an association of work with monetary rewards (most people get paid for work).

Now this definition doesn't encompass all aspects and forms of contemporary work (for example housework or care of children in the family) nor does it focus on the obligatory nature of most work under capitalism. But it does cause us to think about the complex nature of work.

Roberts (1983) talks about a definition of the major elements of leisure which allows exploration of the meaning of leisure as a problem rather than laying down categorically what that meaning is. His three elements are: firstly a type of relatively free or spare time after social, economic, and physiological needs have been met; secondly a type of activity in which play or recreation is an important aspect, separated out from the rest of life by 'time, place and rules'; and thirdly an experience with its own rewards and satisfactions, that is it isn't something we do because we have to or because we get paid for it. Once again, as with Finnegan's definition, it isn't completely ideal nor does it cover every possible situation (some people may not have any even relatively free time, for example) but it does get us out of an impasse for the time being.

The historical context of work and leisure

Finnegan and Roberts both set their definitions quite deliberately in a particular historical and societal context, that of contempoary industrial societies. But of course work and leisure have undergone many historical changes even within a single society. Leisure itself is not simply a product of industrialization, although it is unlikely that those engaged for instance in subsistence farming would have had much 'free time' available to them. But Wilensky (1960) suggests that in the medieval period there were many holidays, possibly as many as one day in three, and Parker (1983) as a result questions whether the relationship between growth of leisure and economic development has been as great as sometimes argued. What is apparent is that in some past societies, for example in the Roman Empire, only a privileged class enjoyed leisure, and such class links have not disappeared. Not only

4

leisure but work too has undergone significant changes over time. These have included the nature of work (for example the shift from agricultural to industrial work, or the development of housework as households and housing have themselves altered), its location (much employment since industrialization has taken place outside the home), organization (the growth of rational and bureaucratic workplaces), the social relationships between workers, how work relates to social inequalities, and the ways in which work is rewarded. In Chapters 2 and 3 I shall be looking more closely at the shape of contemporary work.

In much of the literature on the sociology of leisure there is an assumption that leisure and work are inextricably linked. Burns (1973), in a classic essay, has examined how industrialization, in bringing forward new forms of work and production, also brought forward new forms of leisure and consumption. He points to two particular aspects of this process. Firstly there was the political struggle by industrial workers to wrest free time from the working day, marked in the nineteenth century in Britain by the Ten Hour Act and subsequently by the gradual advent of paid holidays. This perception of leisure as a right, says Burns, came about because since industrialization, work and leisure had come to be seen as increasingly separate in a way not true of pre-industrial life. Employment had come to occupy upwards of seventy hours a week for mid-nineteenth-century factory workers and many saints' days and religious festivals had been suppressed. These struggles not only created a particular form of leisure but also indelibly stamped it with overtones of class and (unrecognized by Burns) gender divisions. The second part of the process which Burns draws attention to was the ways in which leisure under industrialism was 'sanctioned, defined and organized in entirely different terms. The new leisure of the working classes represented a vacuum which was largely filled . . . by amusement industries' (Burns 1973: 45). Commercialization of leisure, closely paralleled by bureaucratization, began to take place, taking in drinking, racing, football, boxing, and newspapers before the end of the nineteenth century, so that consumption of goods and services became part and parcel of leisure.

These processes were clearly very important in shaping leisure in industrial societies. But they tell us only an incomplete story. Although it is true that working-class women were an important part of the industrial workforce, particularly in cotton and textile industries, the fight for leisure as separate from work was a battle waged largely by the male working class. Nineteenth-century women in industrial jobs, whether single or married, were likely to be heavily engaged in housework and childcare. Hence any time not taken up in employment was likely to be spent doing unpaid chores rather than on enjoying commercial leisure. Other occupations commonly done by women such as domestic service were certainly not covered by legislation about hours of work. Middle-class women, unless single, were unlikely to be in employment, and although this meant time for leisure and 'accomplishments' such as music and embroidery as well as supervision of domestic staff, there was, as Hall (1982) has pointed out, none of the much vaunted separation of work and home which was the experience of middle-class males. The work middle-class housewives had to do was, she suggests, more onerous than often thought. Not only this, but the separation of their spouses' work from the home meant that far from engaging in commercialized leisure, middle-class women were cut off from public social life altogether. Women's leisure then was likely even in the nineteenth century to take different forms from that of men, there was less of it because it had to contend more often with the incursion of unpaid work into time free from paid employment, and it was likely to be much more privatized.

In the twentieth century itself changes have continued to affect work and leisure, with the occupational structure altering considerably after both world wars. Developments have been taking place in the design of work, technology, and control over workers and production. There has been

6

increased state intervention in industry, commerce, and employment practices, as well as in industrial relations, and a massive increase in the numbers of married women in employment since the Second World War. Periods of high unemployment have been experienced in the 1930s, 1970s, and 1980s whilst at the same time working hours have gradually reduced and paid holidays have increased for those in jobs. Both in the 1930s and at the present time in the 1980s there have been discussions about the impact of unemployment and reduced working hours on leisure and the prospects of a more leisured society. Strangely the latter still seems a long way off and some of the reasons why will be discussed in the final chapter.

Leisure has also seen changes, from the advent of mass car ownership to the widespread possession of television sets and video-recorders. The public leisure of the 1930s with rambling clubs, uniformed organizations, and ballroom dancing has gradually given way, from the 1950s onwards, to a more privatized leisure existence for men, although no less commercially influenced for all that. Developments in housing (from terraced houses to high rise flats and now back again) and in geographical mobility for job reasons, leaving relatives behind, have helped this privatization. Paradoxically, despite the processes of privatization, the state has also in the twentieth century taken an increasing interest in leisure – whether in controlling the sale of alcohol, regulating the behaviour of football fans, deciding the size of the TV licence fee, building leisure centres, or encouraging people to participate in sport (especially if they happen to be young or unemployed). Neither work nor leisure then has remained static, so our themes are very much in a process of continual change.

Activity

Try to find someone, a neighbour or relative perhaps, who is

over 70 or at least an OAP and talk to them about their own memories of work and leisure in the 1930s, the war, and the 1950s. If you have access to a tape-recorder ask them if you can tape what they say – other students might find it of interest too and it will be easier to talk than if you have to keep breaking off to make notes. Afterwards try to list the changes and differences in leisure and work as they remember them, compared to the present day.

Perspective on work and leisure

Although I will not be spending much time talking about perspectives in this book, it is worthwhile just to look briefly at the main perspectives on work and leisure because these highlight different aspects of the issues which are being addressed here. Now there are of course different ways of doing this. Parker's (1983) well-known text on work and leisure simply divides theorists into segmentalists, who see people's lives as being split into different compartments, each of which operates more or less independently of the others, and holists who perceive society as an integrated whole, where for example leisure and work affect each other and every other sphere of social activity. However, this simple dichotomy actually masks quite complicated theoretical differences, because taking a segmentalist view of leisure does not necessarily mean someone has a segmented perspective on social life as a whole. A more useful way of dividing the perspectives is to do so in the same way as theories are categorized in the discipline as a whole, in the following way.

Functionalist perspectives

This view is close to what Parker calls a holist view, seeing leisure and work as interlocking parts of the social system, each one necessary for the functioning of the whole. Dumazdier (1974) is an example of this approach, with leisure being seen as a way of enabling people to adjust to their social situation without threatening social stability and work as necessary to the smooth functioning of the social system. Conflict is perceived as dysfunctional, so for example people who stayed away from work to play golf or go to the seaside would be considered deviant. Leisure is a means of recuperating from work rather than an alternative to it, except where there is temporary instability (for example in the economic system, leading to unemployment) when it may be used as a work substitute to prevent social unrest.

Pluralist perspectives

Some sociology textbooks suggest, wrongly in my view, that pluralist perspectives are confined to theories about the nature and distribution of power in Western democracies, taking as their main stance the notion of dispersal of power into a large number of different interest groups. Such theories are not however confined to attempts to explain the political system but can also be extended to cover a range of social theorists, including those who write about leisure and work. Both Parker (1983) and Roberts (1983, 1981) are pluralists who see the explanation of leisure and work patterns lying in a considerable number of factors or variables, with no one factor taking priority. Thus Parker, after elaborating the segmentalist and holist approaches outlined previously, then says, 'Both segmentalism and holism appear to be valid to some extent'! Roberts (1981), whilst accepting, for instance that contemporary leisure has in part been shaped by industrialism, rejects the notion that class now plays a major explanatory role and runs through a long list of factors which are thought to influence leisure in some way. There is of course nothing intrinsically wrong with a pluralist approach and many more writers than admit to it actually adopt one, particularly if they are writing about a piece of empirical research. But there is sometimes a lack of a critical explanatory edge.

Weberian perspectives

These are adopted by writers who are particularly concerned to explore the ways in which work, leisure, and sport have become rationalized and bureaucratized over periods of industrialization. So for example Elias and Dunning (1969) suggest that since medieval times leisure pursuits have become increasingly rule-bound (for example football was once an extremely rough game played by whole villages, bearing little resemblance to the modern game) just as work has also become increasingly organized and bureaucratized as part of what they call the 'civilizing process'. This civilizing process has decreased the role of instincts and emotions in human behaviour, although in leisure some aspects of emotions and excitement are retained, in a way which differentiates from work. Later work by Dunning and Sheard (1969) on the development of rugby football looks at the role of sport in controlling violence, as well as exploring further processes of democratization and bureaucratization as they have occurred in sporting activities.

Marxist perspectives

Marxist explanations of the relationship between work and leisure have focused on the role of class relations and the mode of production in shaping leisure and work. Clarke, Critcher, and Johnson (1979) explore leisure as an important part of working-class culture which has been struggled over by industrial workers trying to wrest free time from the owners of the means of production. Although the possibility that employers and the state use leisure as a means of social control is not discounted, leisure is also seen as a way in which the working class can retain some measure of autonomy in a way not possible when they are selling their labour power. Burns (1973), whose essay on the history of leisure in industrial societies was referred to earlier, also has a Marxist perspective on work and leisure.

Feminist perspectives

The major feature of the perspectives already discussed, with the possible exception of pluralism, is that they refer to work as paid employment and that in the main the individuals or groups to which they refer are males. Whilst class features in more than one perspective, gender (and still less race) scarcely gets a mention. A massive literature has grown up over the last two decades documenting the differences between the lives of women as compared with men, although it is only very recently that this literature has encompassed leisure. Although some male theorists are now beginning to acknowledge the importance of unpaid work alongside employment, the full significance of this has yet to become evident in analyses of leisure. Remind yourself at this point of Roberts' (1983) definition of leisure which we used earlier (p. 4). Two of his three elements are time free from obligations and activity marked by different rules, time, and place as play rather than work. For all those women, the majority, who have responsibility for housework and childcare, and also a job, time free from obligations and activities in a way which meets Roberts' criteria is very rare indeed. In my study of women's leisure in Milton Keynes I found only single childless women living alone enjoyed much leisure as defined by Roberts (Deem 1986). Other women combined leisure with domestic responsibilities, gained vicarious enjoyment through their children, and saw such activities as 'taking a nap' as the height of leisure. Feminist perspectives then, whilst not discounting factors like class, see gender relations between women and men in which men assume dominance as having a crucial role in explaining distinctive patterns of female employment, unpaid work, and leisure. Pluralist and Marxist perspectives can incorporate a gender dimension but differ in not giving it prior explanatory importance.

Looking at different perspectives is helpful for what it tells us about current and past debates concerning work and leisure. It is not however particularly useful to use these perspectives to pigeonhole every piece of research or writing on work and leisure that you encounter because you will find this often difficult to do and it will in no way contribute to your understanding of leisure and work.

Researching work and leisure

Studying work and leisure might seem at first fairly easy; much easier, say, than researching the distribution of power or what causes families to fall out with each other. But of course it all depends on what, where and whom you want to research. If you are interested in for example finding out what people earn or what jobs the population of England does, then it is fairly easy to go and find some official statistics – the *New Earnings Survey* or *Social Trends*, published by HMSO and to be found in most libraries, will help you here. Suppose instead you wanted to find out what workers in a particular firm thought about their jobs. You could stand opposite when they leave work and give them a questionnaire (although some of them might tear it up), or if you had their addresses (how would you get them?) you could send it to them. Alternatively you could ask management if you could go inside the workplace and observe the workforce; permission might be refused or if you got access you might find your presence was having what is called the 'Hawthorne effect', that is workers behaving differently just because you are there taking notice of them. Not easy, is it? Indeed getting access to what you want to study can often be more difficult than the actual research; a colleague of mine wanting to study coal mining in India for example found much of his initial visit to India was spent trying to get permission to study the mines rather than getting on with his research as he had hoped. Researchers trying to look at home workers, that is those who are employed to work at home, often on things like making garments or toys for which they receive very low wages, have found those workers understandably reluctant to talk in case they lose even the tiny wage they are getting; studying crime

12

at work or moonlighting usually brings similar problems.

Studying leisure is no more straightforward. In fact it can be more difficult, because while people might be prepared to put up with you watching over them whilst they work, they might be less keen on having you observe a romantic dinner for two or letting you in their house to see what at-home leisure activities they are interested in. Of course, some leisure, like most paid work (we haven't begun to consider unpaid work, which is usually inside people's front doors), is readily visible – pubs, restaurants, leisure centres, cinemas, concerts, sports grounds – but things like knitting, TV watching, stamp collecting, and having friends round for a meal are a little more difficult to close in on. Researching leisure is also more complicated than studying work for another reason too. Most people will know what you mean when you say you are interested in their job or their work; even if it's housework that you are interested in and they don't regard it as 'proper' work they will still know what you mean by the term. Leisure however may not evoke the same ready response in many people. They may think leisure equals hobbies like keeping an aquarium or doing macramé and that therefore it doesn't apply to them because they don't do those kinds of things. They might not equate it at all with watching a video or meeting a friend for a drink. So you have to find more subtle ways of finding out what you want to know – free time, relaxation, enjoyment, non-working time and so on. Of course there are official sources of information on leisure – government publications like *Social Trends* and the *General Household Survey* – but these are also not immune to the same problems an individual researcher faces. A lot of research in the field of leisure has been done through the medium of surveys (usually relying on individual interviews or completion of questionnaires) or just by counting heads (who goes to museums, leisure parks, stately homes, sports centres). But more in-depth studies of leisure have often used long, detailed, and unstructured interviews (that is, where there is no preset list of questions to be asked) or embarked on community studies because leisure is rarely detached from other aspects of people's lives.

Activity

Go to your nearest reference library and see whether they have a copy of the current issue of *Social Trends*, which is published annually by HMSO. There are sections in it on employment and on leisure. Choose one of these to study in a little more detail, and answer the following questions:
1 What are the main sources of this information (usually given at the foot of tables or paragraphs)?
2 Does the information fit with my own experiences and those of my friends and family? If not, why do you think that is – poor methods, your family isn't typical, you live in an isolated community?
3 What sorts of information about work or leisure don't appear there? For example if you wanted to know about what thirty-year-old Afro-Caribbeans or sixty-year-old widows did in their spare time would *Social Trends* help or not? Are there any signs of evidence taken from community studies or research involving workers giving the low-down on why they hate their job?

If you want to know more about research methods, which is a fascinating topic in its own right, then McNeill (1985), in the same series as this volume, is an excellent place to start.

The meaning of work and leisure

One of the things that it is so difficult to get at in research is not what jobs people do or what leisure activities they have but the meanings they attach to those activities. And although interactionists have done research on many areas of social life, they have so far paid little attention to leisure, perhaps because discovering and taping interactions in leisure is much more difficult than, say, it is in a classroom or workplace. Much more attention has been paid to discovering the meanings that work has for people, not only because this is an easier field (though not without pitfalls) to study but also because it has potential economic and social pay-offs (for example in work efficiency).

Parker (1983) suggests that work satisfaction and the meaning of work overlap, in the sense that someone satisfied with their work can see the purpose of that work, whilst someone who is dissatisfied may find their work meaningless, although, as he points out, even in the latter case paid work does have meaning in the sense of providing a living. Berger (1964) is used by Parker to examine a three-pronged analysis of the meaning of work. Berger talks of those whose work provides a major source of self-identity and commitment, those for whom work is a source of oppression, and a third category who are in between these two categories, for whom work is neither very fulfilling nor totally oppressing. Parker suggests that whilst we cannot assume that all middle-class and professional jobs are fulfilling and working-class jobs oppressive, there are three major factors affecting the meaning of work: type of occupation and skill used (although the term skill can cover a huge range of things from technical expertise to socially constructed ways of excluding certain groups of workers), the use to which these skills are put, and finally the status or position within the workplace occupied by an individual. Research on women's employment however (Dex 1985) suggests that employment may provide meaning for women regardless of these factors because it offers financial independence, friends, and an identity not linked just to a house, male partner, and dependent children; gender then is a crucial factor shaping the meaning of work. The unemployed and the retired may also attach to employment a meaning and significance which isn't at all related to having a particular kind of job. As Bocock (1985) notes, in such instances what is crucial is the belief that 'Real people have a paid job'.

15

The meanings attached to unpaid work are also important, although here less research exists. But Oakley's studies of domestic labour (1974, 1976) suggest that whilst childcare can be a source of meaning and satisfaction (although it rarely is if done under conditions of social isolation) housework alone is less likely to provide a lifetime of fulfilment. Social class of course plays a big part here; a middle-class housewife with her own car, friends, activities and voluntary organizations may find her life in general meaningful, with housework just a part of it, whilst a working-class single parent with no transport and little money may find housework and childcare very oppressive.

The meanings attached to leisure have been the subject of almost as much theoretical discussion as actual research. Because there is so much disagreement amongst sociologists about how leisure is defined (much more so than about how work is to be defined) theoretical discussions have tended to take priority. Parker (1983) suggests that what evidence there is links the meaning of leisure firmly to the meaning of work, but of course this gets us back into the problems of defining leisure in relation to time left over after employment. Those for whom leisure time is a scarce resource (for instance women with jobs and domestic responsibilities) may attach more meaning to it than those for whom 'time hangs on their hands' (for instance the retired or the unemployed). But equally there are those who deliberately leave little time for leisure because they find more meaning in other activities (some professionals or obsessively tidy housewives). Since, as we shall see in subsequent chapters, ways of spending leisure vary so enormously, it is much more difficult to make broad generalizations about the meaning of leisure.

Conclusion

I have tried in this introductory chapter to cover a number of issues and debates about work and leisure, focusing on problems of definition, the historical context in which

16

contemporary leisure, employment, and unpaid work have developed in Britain, theoretical perspectives, how leisure and work are researched by sociologists, and the meanings attached to work and leisure. Many of these issues will reappear in later chapters, so don't worry if you aren't yet completely clear about them. What is important is that you have begun to think about work and leisure in ways that extend beyond your own personal experience.

Further reading

A book which covers a number of issues raised here, albeit largely outside the theoretical debates, is Stan Parker's (1983) Leisure and Work *(Allen & Unwin), although, apart from a chapter on housewives, the retired, and the unemployed, the book focuses largely on paid work. On the history of leisure, James Walvin's* Leisure and Society 1830–1950 *(1978, Longman) is an excellent and readable account. Eric Hobsbawm's book* Industry and Empire *(1969, Penguin) covers the history of industrialization in Britain. If you want quickly to revise some of the main theoretical perspectives in sociology, then M. Haralambros' 1985 second edition of* Sociology: Themes and Perspectives *provides a relatively painless way of doing so.*

2

Work in the formal economy

In this chapter the main concern will be to examine some aspects of the sociology of work in the formal economy. Such work, as you saw in the first chapter, is only a part of the work carried out in contemporary industrial societies, albeit an important part. It consists mostly of official paid employment and involves such considerations as the idea of wage labour (that is, the selling of labour power in exchange for wages) and the idea of an employee–employer contract. Until relatively recently virtually all of the sociology of work was concerned only with this kind of work. But increased attention to both work in the informal economy (such as casual employment and 'moonlighting') and to unpaid work (for instance housework) has meant that different kinds of work need to be more clearly distinguished.

Gershuny and Pahl (1985) suggest that it is possible to distinguish three different economies. Firstly there is the formal economy, which encompasses work which goes to make up the official figures of the gross national product.

Secondly there is the hidden or underground economy which involves, just as does the formal economy, the production of goods or services, but unlike in the formal economy work is done either for cash or as part of a system of barter not declared to official taxation or other regulatory authorities. Finally there is the household or communal economy where production (neither for money nor for barter) of goods and services takes place either for the immediate household or in the surrounding community instead of similar goods and services being purchased. So, an example of work in the formal economy would be a job as a secretary; an example in the hidden economy would be a person who mends cars for cash in their back garden, and an example in the household economy would be the making of clothes through sewing and knitting for family members. At one time it was thought that as the formal economy went into recession or experienced no growth, the hidden and household economies would undergo expansion; for example those unable to find employment in the formal economy would turn to producing goods or performing services for cash or barter (for example cooking birthday and wedding cakes for friends and acquaintances). Within the household the unemployed might carry out work which previously would have been paid for and done by someone employed in the formal economy (e.g. rewiring the house). But this view has not been well supported by empirical studies (see Pahl 1984).

Work in the formal economy

What I want to do now is to give you a brief portrait of work in contemporary Britain: the sorts of jobs, who does them and where, and some of the trends in employment over the last two decades. One of the most noticeable trends in the period 1971–1984 is the shift from manufacturing and the heavy industries (e.g. construction, extraction of minerals, etc.) towards jobs in the service sector (for instance banking, finance, commerce, hotels, and the distribution of goods).

19

Other significant changes include a growth in the numbers of married women in employment, from less than one in ten in 1921 to one in two by 1981. There has also been a decline in the economic activity rates of men of employable age, especially in the over 60s age bracket (both as a result of redundancy and of early retirement) and a growth in self-employment and in part-time work (the latter mostly being taken up by women). Changes have occurred in the age at and routes by which young people enter employment, because of new developments in post-school training and education and the raising of the school-leaving age in 1971 and a rise in rates of youth unemployment.

There have also been important changes in state intervention in the economy and employment over the past two decades. These have included anti-discrimination legislation (1975 Sex Discrimination Act; 1965, 1968, 1976 Race Relations Acts; 1970 Equal Pay Act), employment protection legislation (including rights to appear before tribunals in the event of dismissal and maternity leave entitlement), and legislation on industrial relations. The state, particularly in the form of the Manpower Services Commission, has also brought about changes in education and training for jobs, for instance in the shape of the Community Programmes and Job Training Schemes for unemployed adults, the Youth Training Scheme for school leavers, and the Technical and Vocational Educational Initiative for 14–18-year-olds in schools and colleges. The curriculum of schools is also in the process of being changed to a nationally laid down set of guidelines which reflects a concern with vocationally relevant subjects.

There is no space here to enter into a discussion about the economic and social factors lying behind these changes. But what is important is to look at some of the social consequences of the changes in work in the formal economy, not only for employment but also for education, family, and community. The shape of the economy affects who gets jobs, where those jobs are located, what working conditions are like, attitudes to work, and life in the community outside of work. Class structure, linked to economic conditions by all sociologists, also undergoes changes and it is important not to forget the impact on other social divisions like gender, race, and age.

Of course changes in the economy are not confined to the last two decades or even to this century. There has been the cataclysmic impact of industrialization itself, and also the changes in Britain's place in the world economy, initially as head of an empire and a leading industrial nation and then in a less dominant role in a situation where other nations lead in production and the empire has gone. There have been many other significant developments. If we take the period from 1870, then it is possible to pick out changes within types of work as well as in the balance between them. For example during much of the nineteenth century clerical work was a high-status and skilled job done mostly by men. It was still male dominated in 1911, and typewriting was still far from being widespread. But by 1971 the majority of clerical workers were women, many of whom were typists, poorly paid, and regarded as being in fairly low-status jobs. The existence of large numbers of women in the paid labour force in clerical jobs has had important repercussions for households, leisure, family size, and life styles, as well as for the nature of clerical employment and the occupational structure.

Other long-term changes over the last century include a steady decline in the numbers of people involved in agricultural employment (22 per cent of the employed population in 1851, 8 per cent in 1911, 5 per cent in 1951, and well under 3 per cent by the 1980s) and an increase in the size of work organizations (for instance the development of multi-national companies and monopolies and the decline of single family-owned firms). There has also been a related growth in the numbers of managerial, professional, and technical staff compared to manual workers. This has happened both in large organizations (from a ratio of staff to manual workers in British manufacturing of 11.8 per cent in 1924 to 30.2 per cent in 1964) and in the workforce as a whole. So by 1951 clerical workers comprised 31 per cent of those in employment, over double the 1911 percentage, whilst manual work grew by only 6 per cent over the same time period. Although the second half of the twentieth century has seen an enormous increase in service employment, one aspect of it, domestic service, was already in serious decline by the end of the First World War.

Activity

List some ways in which you think changes in work might influence other aspects of social life; for instance the decline in agricultural work has meant more people living and working in urban areas. It has also meant that time, rather than the rhythm of the seasons, has structured employment, that home and job have become separated for more people, and that the countryside has come to be seen by many town-dwellers as a place for leisure rather than as a workplace. It probably makes it easier if you just concentrate on one change. The HMSO publication *Social Trends* will help you with the activity, especially if your local library has some back issues, but don't just look for help in the section on work – try the sections on leisure and education as well, for instance. The further reading for this and the previous chapter will also assist you.

A case study of the social impact of changes in employment

Whilst I'm not going to give you any more help with the activity, going through a case study might help you to see what you are supposed to be getting at. The case chosen is an old one, published in 1969 and known as the Affluent Worker study. It is sometimes called a study of the embourgeoisement thesis (that is, the theory that as working-class people become more affluent they become more like the middle classes in their behaviour, beliefs, attitudes, and voting behaviour) by

Goldthorpe *et al.* You may have come across it in discussions about theories of class. What the study did was to look at a particular group of male employees, Luton car workers, and their families who were at the same time both experiencing and part of a process of social and economic change. During the 1950s and 1960s the car industry was one of the fastest growing sectors of employment, often locating itself in urban areas where new municipal and private housing was being built. Many of those who went to work in the car industry were attracted to it by its high wages and sometimes they left more skilled jobs in order to become relatively unskilled factory workers. In the process most also found themselves moving to a new area, away from their families of origin and kin networks. As the researchers say,

> few of our affluent workers . . . are likely to have found the road to affluence an easy one . . . while in the white-collar world the achievement of higher pay is usually associated with taking on a more complex, autonomous and responsible job, something like the reverse of this has been the typical experience of the manual workers we studied.
>
> (Goldthorpe *et al.* 1969: 60)

What the Affluent Worker study did was to document the instrumental attitude which many car workers had towards their jobs (that is, the jobs themselves were far from enjoyable but were seen as a means by which to achieve a higher standard of living).

In their leisure hours few of the car workers spent time with workmates; their time outside of employment was spent mostly in home-based leisure activities with their families, doing home-related unpaid work activities like DIY (what Gershuny and Pahl 1985 have called the household economy), or more rarely socializing with relatives and neighbours. Over 40 per cent of couples interviewed could name either no or only one or two leisure-time companions. This kind of life style was described by the Luton researchers as a 'privatized' one, contrasted by them with a middle-class life style which

23

would probably have involved a much more outgoing existence and a wider social network than kin or neighbours. The nature of the car workers' jobs, shift work, and in some cases the working of overtime, plus in many cases the move to a completely new area and the absence of significant amounts of leisure time, contributed to this privatization in no small degree. But the social implications of changes in the economy in the 1960s which led to a thriving car industry and well-paid though relatively less skilled and highly supervised jobs for manual workers did not just affect the male workers on whom the study was focused. Not a great deal is said about the wives of the car workers except in so far as they formed part of a couple and were involved in housework and couple-based leisure, although about a third of the wives were said to be in employment (most of those without young children). But think about the position of those wives who were not in employment – stuck in a town where they were new, probably friendless at least initially, with no paid job, and often with demanding small children to look after. 60 per cent of the wives had no close relatives living in Luton and their husbands were often working long hours and maybe shifts too. Their raised standards of living could have been little compensation for their social isolation and unlike their husbands the two-thirds of women not in jobs had no choice about whether they would spend their leisure with workmates, nor did they have their own earnings to spend. You can begin to see then that the social consequences of the kinds of jobs, location of employment, working conditions, and pay which exist in the formal economy have profound implications not only for what happens in the workplace but also for what happens outside the workplace too.

Social divisions in the workforce

The brief discussion about the different experiences of women and men living in Luton brings us nicely to the next issue which is an important part of contemporary sociological

24

thinking about employment. Social divisions are in the simplest sense differences between members of a society which are based not on biological factors (e.g. height or size of feet) but on social factors (for example factory workers rather than doctors). There are a great many social differences in any population but not all social differences are equally interesting to sociologists. Of particular interest are those differences which contribute to the differentiation and integration of society. So for example class divisions both hold society together (for example modern capitalist societies need both employees and employers) and divide it (for instance those who own the means of production and those who have only their labour power to sell may have different interests and may well be in conflict with one another). Such social divisions are also very much concerned with power – those who have power and those who do not. The three most important social divisions in relation to employment are class, race, and gender; traditionally the sociology of work has concerned itself mostly with class and has only recently 'discovered' gender and race, although you should not take this to mean that they are therefore less significant.

Salaman (1985) suggests that there are three ways in which the study of class relates to the study of work. These are inequality, relationships at work, and the dynamics of capitalism. The first two of these apply equally to other social divisions, although the nature of the inequalities and the relationships at work may be different. For example workplace relations between working-class male factory workers and their managers may be conflictual because those relations are based on class; work relations between exploited female secretaries and their male bosses may be difficult because they are based on patriarchy (that is the ways in which men in our society systematically dominate and have power over women); and workplace relationships between black male hospital porters and their white superiors may be conflictual both for class reasons and because of racism.

But just for the moment and so that things don't get so

complicated that it becomes too difficult for you to understand what is being discussed, let's focus just on class and inequality. Inequality based on employment may refer to income differences, job security, working conditions, status, or the content of a job (for example does it involve supervising others or being supervised, does it involve a technical skill like word-processing or using a lathe?). Of course not all differences in work situation or status are class-related; they become so when those differences mark off variations in life chances (what you can reasonably expect to do and be over your lifetime) as well as in the division of labour.

Most theories of class set out empirical or theoretical factors which are seen to divide classes. So for Marx the crucial boundary was between those who sell their labour power and those who buy it and also own the means of production, although subsequent versions have had to grapple with the existence of those workers who undoubtedly sell their labour power but are in managerial positions where they exercise much the same control over other workers as those who own as well as manage the means of production. In Weberian class theories the major divide is on the basis of market situation, that is those whose situation in the labour market is broadly the same (for example all workers with 'A' levels share a market situation; so too do those with no educational or job-related qualifications) and whose value in the labour market is similar. Whereas Marx saw only two major classes, Weber distinguished four – the upper class or those who own property, white-collar workers who own no property, the petty bourgeoisie, and the manual working class.

In both versions of class theory, you can see that jobs and the market for jobs are important factors. In particular, both for these classical versions and for subsequent more sophisticated class theory, there is often a line drawn between jobs which involve manual skill (like road digging or being an electrician) and those which involve mental skill (like being a manager or a solicitor). This line is seen to mark significant differences in market and life chances. A famous study of working-class boys at school by Willis (1977) showed how those (the 'lads') unlikely to get any exam passes hated school and were hard to teach, but looked forward immensely to leaving school and obtaining manual jobs which they associated with being masculine and grown up. Classmates who were academically brighter were looked down upon and called 'earoles'. Not only did these latter enjoy school but they were also destined for what the lads saw as very unmasculine mental jobs in offices rather than hard manual labour in a factory.

There are some difficulties in using the mental–manual divide however, at least as a major part of what differentiates class groups. Firstly, in an economy where there has been a big shift to service industries, it no longer marks a sharp divide in types and conditions of employment. Secondly it applies very much more easily to male jobs than to female jobs. Indeed most theories of class do not really apply to women at all, as Britten and Heath (1983) point out. Recently there has been a fierce debate about the assumption that women can only be attached to classes by virtue of their father's or husband's occupation (see Abbot and Sapsford 1987). Attempts have been made, although there is still no very satisfactory method, to examine women's class position separately from that of men. It is clear from studies of women's employment that whilst there are many manual jobs done by women (for example cleaning and factory work) there are also many non-manual jobs, for example shop work and clerical work where the market situation is very similar, pay and prospects poor, and life chances little different compared with women who do manual work.

Salaman's other two dimensions of class refer to relationships at work and the workings of the dynamics of capitalism. So for example in many forms of employment, relationships between those with similar jobs and the same market capacity are very different to the relationships existing between, for

27

example, managers and shop-floor workers or members of a typing pool. Whilst both forms of relationship may encompass conflict, relationships between managers and their workforce are more likely to display class conflict, particularly over the extent to which managers can control their workforce and the ways in which this control is exerted.

Salaman's third dimension about the dynamics of capitalism refers to the needs of employers to make a profit and the associated necessity therefore to look for ways of cutting costs and making firms more efficient. This means that firms are likely to be organized in a way that benefits managers more than workers and there is a clear class basis to this. So for example a manager might get a pay-rise because he or she has found a way of organizing a firm which involves more use of technology and fewer workers (e.g. the use of robots in car production to do jobs previously done by workers, such as paint-spraying). The workforce however, on the receiving end of this change, might find some of its members facing redundancy as a result of the robots. It used to be assumed that the drive for greater efficiency and profit affected only those in private rather than public sector employment. But moves to privatize parts of the public sector (for instance contracting out hospital cleaning or rubbish collection) and efforts to emphasize value for money in the same sector mean that many public sector employees are now facing similar pressures, although these are not always brought about by their immediate employers.

The labour market at work

Much of the discussion about class and employment refers to market situation and the job market, as you have just seen. Class and capitalism are however not the only factors influencing these. Gender, race, and age also play a part in shaping the market for labour. I have already made several references to something called the job or labour market. Now this isn't the kind of market which sets up its stalls on a Saturday to sell goods to shoppers; indeed it isn't a market which is at all visible. But what it refers to is the sum total of jobs available in a society or in a particular local area, and the relationship between the supply of labour (i.e. how many people are looking for jobs) and the demand for labour (what jobs are available, where, and to whom). This relationship differs according to the state of the economy; for example, in a boom, there may be a huge demand for labour but a small supply of people not currently already employed. In a recession there is likely to be a big supply of unemployed people but a much smaller demand for labour except in very specialized fields. Hence market situation refers to the relative ease or difficulty which an individual or group face in obtaining a job.

Other factors than economic growth affect the labour market; for example state legislation on rates of pay or equal opportunities policies may influence what is available and to whom (e.g. minimum wages for farm workers or the need to interview women and men for job vacancies). Demand for labour then is not a simple matter of jobs being available to anyone. Some jobs recruit only from amongst those already employed in a particular firm (known as an internal labour market) whilst others are open only to those with specialized qualifications. Some groups of workers are able to protect their jobs by laying down who is eligible to join them; for example in the past many jobs in printing were available only to those who were male, were members of a particular union, had served an apprenticeship, and had family or acquaintances already employed in printing (Cockburn 1983). In such instances Freedman (1985) refers to workers erecting a shelter round their jobs and hence affecting the demand for labour, since only a few workers can comply with the conditions necessary for entry. The existence of shelters can lead to what have been called primary and secondary employment conditions. You will perhaps have encountered a version of this theory called the 'dual labour market'. Whilst the divide is

29

rarely as sharply defined in reality as in theory, primary employment conditions are those under which jobs are well paid and relatively secure, where there are usually strong collective bargaining, modern firms, and a predictable demand for products. Secondary employment conditions on the other hand are where the jobs are poorly paid and insecure or temporary, where there is innovation in products, and an unpredictable demand for the product. But it is possible for both sets of conditions to exist in the same firm – for example there may be both permanent workers who are well paid and seasonal temporary workers who are poorly paid. Some occupations do not fit the pattern at all – they may be very well paid but very insecure, as for example with oil-rig workers. So the primary and secondary conditions are approximations and jobs and industries may cluster nearer one or the other.

On the supply side those people available for work are not of course identical either; not only the jobs but the workforce are segmented in various ways. One of the forms of segmentation, class, we have already looked at (compare Willis's 'lads' with the 'earoles'; they have different attitudes, different levels of qualification, and so on). But the labour force is also differentiated by other things, like gender and race and age, which also cross out one another. Those seeking labour are aware of these differences and may under certain economic conditions seek to exploit them, for example by employing young black working-class male school leavers at lower rates of pay than would be acceptable to more experienced white male adults. Disadvantaged groups may be much more likely to end up in secondary employment conditions, particularly if they are women or members of ethnic minorities. This has sometimes been explained by a theory known as the 'reserve army of labour'. This theory argues that, given the tendency for economic conditions to change (from recession to boom, for example), employers may use those who for various reasons are not permanently in a job (women with small children, the unemployed) when they need more workers. When production drops again or the boom ends, they can then dispose of the temporary workers fairly easily. The difficulty with this theory is that it does not explain very well the contemporary patterns of employment for groups like women, in particular the fact that they rarely do, even on a temporary basis, the same jobs as men.

The labour market for women is very different from the one experienced by most men. Women tend to do different kinds of jobs – shop work, secretarial and clerical, light manufacturing, cleaning and catering, the caring professions like nursing or teaching – from the ones done by men, who are found in heavy industry, agriculture, fuel and energy, scientific and technical jobs, and the well-paid professions (e.g. doctors, barristers). Many women are in part-time employment rather than full-time, where the conditions of work and pay are very poor. Part-time workers may have no maternity leave, sick pay, holiday or pension entitlement, particularly in Britain (as compared to other EEC countries). Over 90 per cent of part-time workers are female. Even in full-time employment, despite legislation on equal pay, women's wages remain less than 80 per cent of men's in most fields of employment, and women predominate in the lower rungs of many jobs and organizations. There are many debates about why women are disadvantaged in the labour market – discrimination, lack of commitment to employment, household and childcare responsibilities, lack of geographical mobility in their own right unless they are single, unwillingness to apply for promotion, absence of relevant qualifications, and so on (Dex 1985). Nevertheless, it is worth pointing out that recent British research (Martin and Roberts 1984) notes that most women, whether married and mothers or not, are spending much more of their adult life in employment than they did even two decades ago. Although many take a break for childbirth and may then return to part-time or lower-status employment than previously, the breaks taken for childrearing are getting shorter and many women now return to employment in between the births of their children, rather than remaining out of employment for the whole of the time that they are having and bringing up young children.

The difficulties experienced by members of ethnic minorities in obtaining jobs are also hotly debated – is it racism, lack of qualifications, being located in urban areas where there are few jobs, etc? The evidence available does seem to suggest in the case of both women and ethnic minorities, that discrimination and unequal power relations (not just between workers or would-be workers and their employers, but also between male white workers and women and ethnic minority workers) based on patriarchy (male dominance over women) and racism (certain, usually majority, groups exercising power over other, usually minority, groups on the false premise that some ethnic groups are biologically and socially inferior to other groups) are major factors which contribute to women's and ethnic minority groups' subordinate position in the labour market (West 1982, Dex 1985 on gender; Smith 1981, Braham, Rhodes, and Pearn 1981, Troyna and Smith 1983 on race). Ethnic minority groups tend to occupy jobs with low pay, little security, and few possibilities of promotion. But we need to be careful here to realize that we cannot explain the position of, say, black workers just by reference to racism and ethnic disadvantage; class and gender also need to be taken into account. So a black working-class woman may find it much more difficult to obtain a well-paid secure job than a middle-class black man, although both are likely to experience racial harassment in the course of their recruitment and employment.

Activity

Get hold of a local paper for the area in which you live. Study the adverts for jobs. What sorts of jobs are advertised? Try to see if you can categorize them as primary and secondary jobs. It's illegal for most employers to advertise jobs for one sex only; but see if you can guess who is expected to apply for jobs like 'security guard – must be strong' or 'secretary wanted – pleasant manner'. What do the job adverts tell you about the jobs available in your area? Are there lots of jobs or hardly any? Is this related to the unemployment rate? What sorts of employers and firms are advertising – big firms, local government, etc? Also try to find out from other sources – the library, parents, friends, Trades Council, Chamber of Commerce, etc – what the main local industries and jobs are. This will help to give you a picture of your local labour market to compare with the national picture discussed here. A recent national census on employment (1984 Census of Employment, published 1987) has revealed a sharp national division in employment, with jobs growing in the South East, South West, and East Anglia but many job losses in the North East, North West, Scotland, Wales and the Midlands. See if you can find out which category your area is in – north or south, many new jobs appearing, or many job losses. What effect do you think this regional divide has on the market for labour in general? What effects does having lots of jobs in an area have on other things, like the price of houses or how much it costs to buy food? Why should there be regional differences in employment patterns and why can't people just move to where the jobs are?

The deskilling of employment

I want next to explore briefly some other directions taken by debates about the sociology of work which are both important in themselves and also have implications for the study of leisure. One of the most important contributions to the discussion about how capitalism influences employment has been made by Braverman, in his book *Labor and Monopoly Capital* (1974). What Braverman considers in the book is how capitalism has shaped the form of work in its search for greater efficiency and profits. Braverman suggests that the efforts of the American F.W. Taylor (in a book about scientific management first published in 1912) have been very important in shaping the subsequent organization of work. What Taylor did was to argue that efficiency is best achieved by separating out the design of tasks (for example how a table should be made) and their execution. Managers should decide what was to be done and workers would carry out their instructions, thus ensuring the maximum prosperity of both workers and managers. The application of Taylorism, as it has become known, to factory work resulted in tasks being broken up into tiny parts, with each worker responsible for only one or two of these parts (for example putting rivets on a part of a car) and hence having a monotonous job, closely supervised and paced (the latter by the speed of the assembly line) without any autonomy or individual worker decision-making being necessary or possible. Braverman argues that variations on Taylorism have increasingly been applied to all jobs; that is tasks have been broken down into tiny components and 'deskilled' so that they are easy to do but very boring and allow no scope for individual ability or initiative. This process has been helped by the development of technology which reduces the need for workers to possess any technical skill (for example the invention of the typewriter reduced the need for clerical workers to have beautiful handwriting). All control is thus in the hands of managers. Labour power and those who sell it are subordinated completely.

Braverman saw the process of deskilling affecting not just manual jobs like factory work, but also many white-collar jobs too. Contemporary analyses of some jobs suggest that indeed the technical content and autonomy required are minimal; in a study of unskilled jobs in Peterborough, Blackburn and Mann (1979) suggest that most workers used more skill driving to work than they used at work. Studies of clerical and secretarial workers (Crompton, Jones, and Reid 1982) suggest that technological changes like computerization have also deskilled those jobs and made them monotonous and lacking in autonomy. Cockburn (1983) in her study of technological and other changes in the printing industry also relates how those changes have made it difficult for printers to maintain the previous mystique which existed about the nature and difficulty of their work. Changes in the way newspapers are produced for example have made it possible for anyone who can use a typewriter or computer keyboard to take on jobs previously done by printers alone, such as typesetting and compositing. But printers, as Cockburn points out, had long used the so-called technical skills of their jobs to retain conditions of primary employment for themselves, keeping out so-called undesirable labour like women workers, and now can no longer keep out those who have not been through long apprenticeships.

However, as Salaman (1986) has pointed out, whilst no-one denies that some deskilling has taken place, it has not been a uniform process nor have workers placidly accepted managerial control and reduced skill and autonomy (take for example the demonstrations of sacked print workers outside Rupert Murdoch's Wapping newspaper plant in 1986 and 1987). Not all factory work, possibly the easiest to deskill, has been organized according to Taylorist principles and some car manufacturers, for example, have experimented with groups working on producing just one car at a time. Other changes, for example computerization, have led to the creation of new skilled jobs or added additional skills (for example a secretary using a word-processor to record and retrieve data as well as for typing documents) rather than simply taking away previous skills. Also the question of what skill is, isn't straightforward, as women workers in Britain and America in the Second World War showed. Working in heavy industries they were able to do things like welding with scarcely any training when previously it had taken several years of apprenticeship to do the same task. (If you are interested in exploring this last point further, the film *Rosie the Riveter* is about American women war workers. Your tutor may be able to get it for you.) Whilst some tasks obviously require technical skill, the notion of a skill has also been socially constructed so that something appears more difficult than it is as a way of protecting or sheltering certain kinds of jobs. This has particularly been done by male workers and certain male-dominated trade unions. Thus only some workers (for example those who have served an apprenticeship) are eligible to enter a particular job. What all this tells us is that there is no simple way in which capitalism, or socialism either for that matter, determines the forms of work which exist in contemporary industrial societies. Also, although deskilling work is one way in which managers can control their workforce, there are other ways too in which that control can be exercised. Salaman (1986) suggests that what the sociology of work has done, in concentrating so much on Braverman's deskilling thesis, is to ignore many aspects of individual and group experience in employment and forget about things like the meaning of work.

Activity

It is difficult to decide what a skill is; but just try to write down a couple of examples of one (e.g. riding a bike, making a dress, mending a car). Why do you think people might try to suggest that something is more difficult to learn than it actually is? Would this apply more when it's a work skill rather than something you might do at home? Think back to the beginning of this chapter and the discussion about the formal, informal, and household economies. Some of the same skills (e.g. cooking, fixing a car) are used in all three; but in the formal economy it will often be expected that there's been some formal training. Is this always necessary? Has it always been necessary – is there more emphasis on training for jobs now for instance? If there is, doesn't this suggest deskilling is a bit too simple – why bother to train anybody if most jobs are now deskilled?

Take something you regularly do – perhaps writing an

essay or painting and decorating or mending your bike or motorcycle or baking a cake – and see how many stages you can break it down into. If there were five people carrying out the same task – e.g. writing a very long essay – and you were in charge, how would you divide it up? Would you give everyone three lines on every page to write, for instance, or get someone to research the topic, someone else to design the shape of the essay, a third to write it, and a fourth to type it neatly? You can begin then to appreciate that breaking tasks into tiny parts isn't the only way to organize work, nor necessarily the most successful.

Social relations in the workplace

I want to finish this chapter by looking at an example of how Salaman (1986) suggests the sociology of work might develop in directions different from those taken by the deskilling thesis. There is not enough space to go into this issue in detail, but one way Salaman himself has researched social relations in the workplace is in a study of attempts to implement Equal Opportunities policies, particularly the employment of women firefighters, in the London fire brigade. The difficulties experienced in trying to bring about equal opportunities in employment are sometimes seen (and remember in Britain this is a very recent topic) as being attributable solely to discrimination and prejudiced attitudes. So for example if women firefighters aren't welcomed then this is because male firefighters have prejudiced views about women in employment – they think women should stay at home looking after housework and children, or that women haven't the physical strength and stamina to fight fires. Now in part it was the case that many of the firemen Salaman talked to did have such views. But to stop here, with just attitudes of the existing workforce, would be to fail to understand both other aspects of the difficulties experienced in trying to implement Equal Opportunities policies and why male firemen have such a chauvinistic culture. As Salaman notes, workplaces contain both formal and informal structures, and what is formally supposed to happen, like admitting women firefighters, may be very different from what actually happens, for reasons which are rarely foreseen at the outset.

Recruitment to the fire service has always been highly selective, with many applicants turned down, and so in the London Fire Brigade much emphasis was placed on informal methods of recruiting, mainly through contacts of already serving firefighters. Consequently most of those actually recruited came from very similar backgrounds to those already employed, although each one also had to pass demanding selection tests. So most were white working-class men and the solidarity this recruitment process introduced was intensified by the way in which fire brigade work is organized. Firefighters are organized in watches which are groups of people who are in the fire station at the same time. They do not merely work together, but in between fighting fires share jokes, leisure interests which could be used to while away any time in the station on watch, and a general companionship. They thus develop a sense of camaraderie, based on shared in- and out-of-work experiences and the knowledge that they are a highly selected group. The firemen in the study were not closely controlled by their superior fire officers; indeed discipline and control sometimes rested on very informal relations. But the firemen deeply distrusted their senior officers; although promotion through the highly structured ranks was theoretically very open, many firemen resented not having been promoted. The introduction of criteria like positive discrimination (i.e. relying on more formal methods of recruitment and positively seeking out suitable applicants who were also women or black) into the fire service in 1981, rather than just merit and in practice being like the existing firemen, was seen as greatly reducing white men's promotion chances. It was also seen as disturbing (where it involved the recruitment of women firefighters) the all-male solidarity of the watches and introducing firefighters who were inferior and unable to do the job properly.

The attempts to introduce an Equal Opportunities policy then met with not only sexist attitudes from firemen but also introduced completely different recruitment methods. The policy was seen to threaten male promotion and was also considered inimical to fighting fires properly because in part this last depended on good team relationships existing between members of the same watch. To understand this process is not to say that the firemen were right to dislike the Equal Opportunities policy. But it does show that the nature of informal work groups, the meaning work has for individuals, and the extent of shared backgrounds and leisure interests are important in understanding what happens in the formal economy. Think back to the earlier case study of the Luton car workers. They had a completely different work situation, with no work group solidarity at all and very little contact between workers outside of their working hours. But it would not be possible to understand the lives of those car workers, nor the meaning or lack of it which their work had for them, without going beyond the nature and form of their work.

Conclusion

In this chapter I have tried to cover a number of important debates and issues about employment in contemporary Britain but at the same time tried to convey a picture of what kinds of work exist in the formal economy. Remember that this hasn't involved just studying work in isolation, but has also helped you to consider how leisure and work are connected. So we not only need to understand how employment is organized but also what it means to the individuals concerned, who works with whom, who finds getting a job difficult, who doesn't get paid much, and so on. Hence learning about changes in the economy, about the social implications of economic change, about divisions in the workforce, about how the labour market works, about deskilling and about the importance of informal as well as formal aspects of work organization and relationships will help you in due course to understand why social divisions and meaning, for example, are vital to an understanding of work and leisure. It will also assist you to grasp why those who are unemployed might perceive leisure differently from those who are employed. You should also be starting to understand that the sociology of employment is not just about class, as many textbooks would have you believe, but also about gender and race and other social factors too. In the next chapter we shall be looking at work outside the formal economy, including unpaid work, trying to see how such work differs from that done in the formal economy and what social implications this has.

Further reading

An American book which gives accounts of people describing their working lives and which you might find useful as a basis for doing some analysis of your own is S. Terkel's Working *(1983, Penguin).*

A British and more overtly sociological version of this is to be found in C. Littler, The Experience of Work *(1985, Gower). More demanding, but worth it if you are interested in theories or in learning more about the fire brigade research, is G. Salaman's little book* Working *(1986, Ellis Horwood).*

3

The hidden economy and unpaid work

In this chapter I want to look a little more closely at forms of work which are generally regarded as being outside the formal economy. If you remember back to the beginning of Chapter 2, I mentioned how Gershuny and Pahl (1985) distinguish between two different aspects of the informal economy, the *hidden* or *underground economy* which covers work or production 'wholly or partly for money or barter, which should be declared to some official taxation or regulatory authority, but which is wholly or partly concealed', and the *household economy*, where goods and services are produced, 'not for money, by members of a household and predominantly for members of that household . . . for which approximate substitutes might otherwise be purchased for money'. So an example of the underground economy might be a gas fitter who uses the firm's tools and van after hours to connect gas fires for cash and 'no questions asked'. An example of the household economy would be the cooking of meals by someone in the household, perhaps a parent, when if this was not done meals would have to be purchased in a café.

But this categorization does not exhaust all kinds of work outside the formal economy. Sometimes work done in the home is performed because there is no commercial or state-provided alternative – for instance care of infirm but not acutely ill old people. Certain sorts of paid work which are done at home are on the margins of the formal economy; a woman making Christmas crackers for a commercial organization for a rate per cracker is often counted as self-employed, so that the employer doesn't have to pay national insurance contributions. However, she may have to work long hours to earn even a small amount of money, which is too small to be taxed. Such arrangements are sometimes illegal and if so then the work is part of the hidden economy. This is vastly different from someone who runs a business at home but complies with all the regulations about tax, national insurance, and so on, who would count as part of the formal economy.

Activity

1 Make a list of all the kinds of work you can think of which might be part of the hidden or household economy. Put them in columns like this:

Hidden economy

mending cars for cash only
using office typewriters to
    type a novel for a friend

Household economy

making a dress
decorating a room

Are there some types of work which go in both columns (e.g. you can mend your own car at home for nothing except the cost of parts or get your neighbour to do it whilst you pay them for their labour and the parts)? Are there any which only go in one? How many types might also go in the formal economy under different conditions (e.g. taking your car to a garage instead of mending it yourself or getting a neighbour to do it)?

2 Ask someone else, with your help, to think of all the sorts of work they might do in a week which aren't part of a regular paid job; if you have time ask a man and a woman and compare the different lists. Ask them to include things like a second job (and remember to say you'll keep things confidential or they might not include everything!). Compare their work lists with the one you did in the first part of the activity, thinking about the following points as you do so:

- What kinds of things, if any, did your list exclude and theirs include?
- If you were able to ask a man and a woman, are there any substantial differences in the kinds of work mentioned (e.g. cooking meals as against mending the car)?
- How much time do the people you asked seem to have left for leisure? A lot or a little?

3 Keep a detailed diary for two days; write down everything you do, from getting up to going to sleep, and the time. Then for each thing try to decide whether it is work (formal, hidden, household) or leisure. This method is often used by sociologists to study the balance between work and leisure or between different kinds of work. What particular advantages and disadvantages might it have as a way of finding out what work and leisure people do? Did you find it difficult to keep such a diary? Are there things you deliberately left out? If you did two things at the same time – for instance eating your tea and watching TV – did you write both down?

The information gleaned from these activities suggests that it isn't always easy to decide what kinds of work fit where. Nor are the ways in which sociologists find out about these things without their pitfalls.

43

The informal economy – growth or decline?

Although there is no space here to delve into a history of work outside the formal economy, the kinds of work discussed are of course not themselves new. Community studies and other evidence over the last hundred years indicate that such a distinction has been with us a long time, even if it is only comparatively recently that sociologists have developed concepts and theories to explain it. When research into the informal economy began to become an important part of the sociology of work in the late 1970s, there tended to be an assumption that as the formal economy shrank (the process is also sometimes called deindustrialization), whether through the closure of firms and factories, through shorter hours of employment, or lower wages, or through unemployment, so the hidden economy would grow. So when the Gershuny and Pahl (1985) article was first published in 1980 (I have used the later date because it is in a book and so easier to track down than the journal where it first appeared) this assumption was quite widespread. As Pahl wrote in 1978

> it is also now possible for people to get by without necessarily engaging in formal employment. A man can own his own tools . . . he can control much of his time . . . and the state provides a long-stop to prevent starvation with its unemployment and social security benefits. Far from the immiseration of the workers which Marx predicted, welfare capitalism may have handed back to some the ownership of the means of production: there is a market demand for craft skills, and there are ways of avoiding paying taxes . . . . Preliminary interviews with 'unemployed' men . . . have led me to think that the incentives for some skilled workers to remain unemployed in a formal sense outweigh the advantages of a regular wage.
>
> (Pahl 1984: 10)

Subsequently Pahl's researches on the Isle of Sheppey suggested that regular wages and jobs do have significant advantages over other forms of paid work and that unemployment may actually make it difficult to engage in the hidden economy because there is little money for tools and fewer social contacts, who themselves have a regular adequate income, from whom to derive work.

Following his more recent empirical research, Pahl in 1984 suggested that the hidden economy might actually be in decline, and gave five reasons for this:

- The self-employed are a group with a long tradition of under-reporting of their actual incomes and profits according to the tax authorities. Evidence available between 1975 and 1979 suggested that self-employment was in decline (although by 1984 it had started to grow again according to *Social Trends* 1985).
- Unemployment increases reduce the possibilities available for using the workplace as a base for hidden work and a source of information, tools, and contacts.
- By the 1980s the unemployed were under increased surveillance from neighbours and official DHSS investigators all looking for evidence of individuals simultaneously receiving state benefits and earning money from other sources.
- More efficient and vigilant tax inspectors particularly focusing on the hidden economy.
- The growth of what Pahl calls self-provisioning by households, that is where members of a household provide for themselves services or goods like DIY or gardening or car maintenance.

It isn't possible to answer this question of growth or decline in the short term but it does illustrate, I think, how much easier it is to study and therefore to measure the formal than the informal and household economies.

What counts as the hidden economy?

Finnegan (1985b) argues that there are three main aspects of

45

the hidden economy – illegal work like professional burglary; non-reported work such as having a second job or working for payment from home but not reporting it to the Inland Revenue; and unofficial perks, fiddles, and pilfering from official paid work and workplaces. It is at this point that we realize that the term hidden economy refers not just to certain kinds of work under particular conditions, but also to material gains, not necessarily just monetary ones, of a hidden or underground kind (for instance taking home writing paper from the office to use to write to your relatives or using the firm's car and petrol to go to the seaside for the day or pretending that you are ill whilst actually doing your Christmas shopping). The state is also crucially important to definitions of the formal and hidden economies because state social and economic policies and legislation, as well as the organization of things like taxation and national insurance, are a major determinant of what counts as the formal economy and what remains 'hidden'. So, too, are the criteria and ways in which unemployment statistics are compiled. So a society with relatively little direct taxation (as through deductions from wages or salaries) will also have less evasion of that taxation, something which is a major factor in unreported work. Furthermore some forms of work which are illegal under British law are legal in other countries (prostitution is one example).

Illegal work

This covers, in the main, work which is illegal not only because it isn't declared to the Inland Revenue, but because the very nature of the job contravenes the law. Examples of illegal work would be making a living from thieving or receiving stolen goods, working as a prostitute, dealing in drugs, or pretending to be a travel agent taking money for holidays but not actually providing any holidays. Precisely because this kind of work is illegal, it is impossible to estimate its extent in any society. There is also a fine line between some forms of unreported work and illegal work. As Finnegan (1985b) indicates, illegal work is only rarely studied by sociologists of work and more usually by those interested in deviance or criminology, although it is clearly of interest to both. Terkel (1983), for example, includes only one type of illegal work, prostitution, in his extensive set of interviews with Americans in a wide variety of work. Littler (1985) includes only theft and larceny as 'sidelines' to legal employment rather than as occupations in their own right. Yet many of the ways in which employment is analysed are equally applicable to illegal work. Gender and power relations, definitions of sexuality, and state legislation are extremely necessary to an understanding of why prostitution exists and why some women 'choose' to earn a living in this way. Mechanisms of control and hierarchies of workers, social relationships between workmates, and issues to do with social class are just as much part of organized theft as they are of factory work.

Unreported work

There are, as I have indicated already, aspects of unreported work which are illegal, even if the nature of the work itself is not illegal. Thus, it is not illegal to take in lodgers or do typing at home or charge others 'cash in hand' to decorate their house, but it is illegal not to declare such earnings to the Inland Revenue. Similarly it isn't illegal to mend other people's cars at your house or to connect gas cookers for friends – but having a car repair business at home may contravene planning laws and connecting gas cookers may break gas safety regulations. Both these latter forms of work may also depend on the unauthorized use of an employer's tools outside of working hours. There are typically three kinds of people who do unreported work: those who already have some legal employment and who are 'moonlighting' or taking a second job; those who are formally unemployed or retired and in receipt of state benefits; and those who have neither a job nor receive state benefits, but who use an unreported job as a source of independent and sometimes vitally necessary money, for instance full-time housewives.

It is important to see unreported work not just as something resulting from individual decisions, but as closely related to ideologies, social divisions, state policies, and social institutions. Those who take second jobs may be earning low wages, perhaps because they are unskilled members of the working class, women, or from an ethnic minority group (Alden 1981). Or they may do their unreported work for social reasons, to help out friends or relatives in a difficult situation (unemployment, sickness, and so on). Someone who dislikes their full-time job may find identity and satisfaction in their second job, doing something they enjoy and which they, not someone else, control, as with a factory worker who grows and sells fruit and vegetables from their allotment in their spare time. Finnegan (1985b) also suggests that some tasks, like window cleaning, bar work, and taxi driving, which involve either unsocial hours or low earning potential, might not get done except when done by someone as a second job.

An important category of unreported work is homeworking, which is not the same thing as doing casual work like repairing cars from home, but is work done for an employer at home rather than in an office or factory. Homeworking and outworking are not always unreported, but the nature of the work (often it involves piecework like making garments, toys, or fancy-goods items), the frequently extremely low wages, and the fact that employers are sometimes utilizing home-workers illegally or under conditions which they would never get away with in a conventional workplace mean that they are often unreported. Many homeworkers are women, often with young children to care for and unwilling or unable to find a job outside the home but needing a source of income, however low.

Both women and men are involved in unreported work. Indeed in our society the taxation position of married women (whose earnings are still mainly taxed as though they were appendages of their husbands, even to the extent of their husbands filling in their earnings on his tax form) positively encourages non-reporting, particularly by women who want some money which is independent of and unknown to their husbands. The 1980 Women and Employment survey (Martin and Roberts 1984) found that women in part-time employment were more likely to have a second job than women in full-time jobs, whereas the pattern for men is the reverse (that is, it is mostly men in full-time jobs who have second jobs). Unemployed people and the so-called 'economically inactive' (this includes those who have retired) may also be involved in unreported work.

As with illegal work, it is difficult to discover the extent of second jobs and unreported work and it can be hard to research. Pahl (1984) found that whilst people were happy to talk about their unreported and illegal work to him whilst he sat in cafés and houses in Rochester, and later when he and Claire Wallace were doing similar research on the Isle of Sheppey, there were ethical problems about writing up such studies. Those trying to research poorly paid women home-workers have encountered similar problems.

Pilfering, fiddling, and job perks

I have deliberately left this until last because it is much less central to a consideration of work and leisure than either illegal or unreported work. Nevertheless, pilfering from an employer or exploiting the perks of a job (whether it is access to tools and equipment or using an expense account for holidays rather than meeting business colleagues) do offer a source of extra wages or benefits and may help individuals to put up with unsatisfying employment or poor wages and conditions or even enjoy a leisure pursuit not otherwise possible (e.g. someone who works in a sports shop may by 'borrowing' sports equipment be able to take up a sport they could otherwise not afford).

Mars (1985) in a study of pilfering by hotel employees argues that pilfering is so widespread in some occupations that it is considered part of the job. The methods used by some of the people Mars studied are indeed ingenious:

In lounges serving coffee and tea, fiddling is often extremely simple. A waiter receives an order for, say, two coffees. He goes to the kitchen, orders a single coffee . . . he obtains a standard coffee pot, standard milk jug and one cup and saucer. The problem is to convert this single coffee to two coffees . . . extra cups and saucers . . . are frequently hidden in strategic areas in or near the lounge. Crockery may be kept behind a flower display, behind curtains, even carried in pockets . . . A waiter's second requirement is for strong enough beverages; coffee and tea ordered for two may be too weak if served to three. This often requires a 'bent' helper in the kitchen . . . usually repaid in beer, rarely in cash.

(Mars 1985: 264–5)

Of course pilfering is not always as organized as this and may involve something as simple as someone filching biros from the office to give to their children. Ditton's (1974) research on fiddling by bread sellers even indicates that employers and supervisors may know what is going on and 'turn a blind eye' in the belief that they are thereby preventing more serious theft and crime.

The exploration of work in the hidden economy not only allows us to look at another aspect of people's lives, but also shows how limited would be a sociology of work which looked only at work in the formal economy. Equally an analysis of work and leisure which focused only on paid legal employment and leisure would miss important dimensions and activities which take place in the spaces between those two categories, but which are just as relevant to understanding the network of social relationships people possess, the beliefs and attitudes they have, and how they use their time. I now want to go on to look at unpaid work in the household.

Work in the household economy

If unrecorded and illegal work have not always been accorded their due significance, this is even more the case with the work which takes place, for the most part unpaid, in the household economy. Yet without such work, which covers a wide range from cleaning to house painting, work in the formal economy would be much more difficult and the state or employers, or both, would have to provide a much wider range of services than is usually on offer in capitalist societies. Workers would turn up for work having eaten nothing since their canteen lunch the day before, in dirty clothes, and with small children in tow. The goods and services not provided in the household would also have to be paid for if they were to come from other sources. Household labour is not usually costed, even though of course there is still a monetary element, unless a household is completely self-sufficient (such as the cost of food or cleaning materials). Nevertheless, as Maynard (1985) notes, the family is a unit within which people make economic decisions about paid and unpaid work in the household and outside it. For example the decision of a mother not to return to work after the birth of a baby may be based as much or more on the low wages she is likely to earn and the high cost of childcare, as on the belief that mothers should stay at home with their children.

Activity

Imagine you are going to live entirely on your own in a self-contained flat in a strange town where you know nobody. You have a job from 8.30am to 5.30pm (there is no canteen at the workplace) but otherwise no other formal commitments. Write down all the things you will need to do for yourself or to purchase if you are going to remain well fed, clothed, in a clean flat. Next write beside these who does them at present and whether this costs money or not. For instance, if you lived

51

alone you'd have to do your own washing or pay someone to do it for you at a laundry or launderette. But at the moment maybe your mother, husband, or flatmate does your washing for you free of charge. When you've done this extend your imaginary solitude to include a four-year-old child. What tasks and work does this add and how would you cope with these? You might like to do this as a group exercise, giving each person or pair of people a slightly different imaginary situation (e.g. living with an elderly frail dependant; living with a husband or wife and two children; sharing a flat with a friend). The activity will certainly give you some insights into just how much unpaid work there is in everyone's lives, either done by them or done for them by someone else.

The extent of the household economy at any one point depends on a whole number of factors, including the economic situation and policies of the state. In periods of high economic growth when there is a need for workers which almost outstrips the supply, services like nurseries may be more readily available than they are at times of high unemployment (for instance in the 1960s in Britain many middle-class married women were encouraged to re-enter the labour market, particularly into jobs like teaching, and the amount of state childcare provision and special training schemes for married women returners increased). In times of war, too, arrangements have been made to feed more people in cafés and to care for young children outside the home.

Housework

The growth of the contemporary feminist movement in Britain drew particular attention to women's work in the household and to its role in giving women who were housewives a subordinate status, without a wage or recognition. Much attention has been paid to the economic value of domestic labour, something which is referred to as the domestic labour debate, and which Marxists have been particularly interested in. But that debate in itself does not really tell us much about the nature of housework nor even who does it. Housework has long been seen as the preserve of women although it really only became separated from other forms of work when industrialization took some forms of work outside the home into factories and shops and offices and at the same time family life began to be developed as a sphere separated from paid work and its rigours. The process of change was, as Maynard (1985) points out, certainly not as smooth as might be thought. Even within England there were regional and class variations. In the textile industries of northern England for example in the late eighteenth century and early nineteenth century, some working-class women moved into factory and mill work in the same way as men, rather than men going out to work and the women staying at home to do housework. Other women remained at home but made garments on an outwork basis. Elsewhere middle- and upper-class women had servants to do their domestic labour and only supervised its carrying out. In the nineteenth century increasing attention came to be paid to childcare as well as care of the house and its adult occupants. Maynard notes that it was not only housework itself and the role of women in performing such work which developed considerably in the nineteenth century but also a set of ideas about domesticity. The most important of these ideas were images of womanhood and the ideal home. Women were seen as biologically and culturally different from men. Their job was to create and preserve a domestic haven for their husbands and children (Davidoff 1976) using high standards of housekeeping and cleanliness. Elements of this ideology have persisted until the present day, despite an increasing involvement of large numbers of mothers and married women in paid employment for much of their adult lives.

One of the problems about examining housework from a sociological viewpoint is to decide what it consists of, as well as determining who does it. So for example do we count decorating and painting as well as cooking and washing clothes; is maintaining the car the equivalent of keeping the house clean? Such arguments have more than superficial significance because the extent to which housework reflects a rigid or more equitable division of labour is very much bound up with what is included under the heading. Thus Oakley (1974), Malos (1980), and Maynard (1985) indicate that women are continuing to carry most of the burden of domestic labour, whereas other analyses suggest that men are doing much more around the house, perhaps as a consequence of women's greater involvement in paid employment (Gershuny and Jones 1987).

Housework generally is understood to include things like cooking, shopping, cleaning, washing of clothes and household items, caring for children and dependants (e.g. sick or disabled household members), and other tasks associated with running a house on a daily basis. Since the running of a house also includes in many cases keeping it in good repair, work like gardening and DIY might reasonably be included. Other activities like repairing cars are more problematic, since often vehicles are used mainly by the person who owns them, although the household at large may use a car from time to time. Housework, as Delphy (1984) has pointed out, is not the same as the work individuals have to do for themselves (think back to the last activity) but is work which services other members of a household and/or family. It is this element of serving others and the typical gender and power relationships under which housework often takes place (usually regarded as a housewife caring for her male partner and children, although of course there are also those forms of housework done by single parents, adult children caring for elderly parents, childless couples, and house- or flatmates) as well as the ideology surrounding who should do housework which ensure that the performance of the housework is often full of contradictions and conflicts. Maynard (1985) outlines five possible sources of these:

54

- The ideology that housework is non-work is still a pervasive one. This is partly because it is seen as a set of easy tasks with no boss or set hours; as one housewife said of her husband's reaction to her idea that housework is indeed work: 'Joe tells me I am freer than he is – I can do things in my own time without any pressure from anybody' (Gail, in Littler 1985: 184). But the conditions under which housework takes place for many working-class women are no better than a factory – cold houses and flats, little money, screaming children, few pieces of household equipment – and although there is no wage to be deducted for poor performance or a boss to shout, husbands are often very critical of housekeeping standards (Oakley 1976). Housework is work but it is work with little status attached to it and it is done for love or because of emotional and financial ties. The view that housewives do housework in return for a home and an income provided by a male breadwinner is dying out only slowly despite the fact that most women can now expect to be in employment for most of their adult lives.
- Housework has no set routines – but many housewives set their own very demanding ones and this can bring about an obsession with housework. Oakley (1976), Yeandle (1984), and Sharpe (1984) all found women who washed their household's clothes by hand rather than use a machine because they felt the clothes looked better and wore longer.
- Women do like the sense of autonomy housework gives them, although it is a very different type of autonomy to that experienced by someone who lives alone, because there are other members of the household around some of the time. Oakley (1976) found that cooking and shopping were the most popular tasks, the first because it can be creative and the second because it offers a chance to get out of the house. But many women feel they have to ration the enjoyable tasks in order to do the less pleasant ones and self-imposed routines may reduce freedom rather than increase it.

- Children also inspire housewives with contradictory feelings. On the one hand children are seen as one of the most enjoyable aspects of housework, but on the other it is often children, their needs, and demands, which make housework difficult to carry out and never-ending in terms of its tasks. I found this dual view of children very prevalent amongst the women I talked to in my Milton Keynes research on leisure – children were both a source of pleasure and relaxation and a burden whose care destroys leisure time and the possibility of non-family leisure (Deem 1986).
- A sizeable minority of housewives express considerable dissatisfaction with their work. As one housewife said to Yeandle (1984: 96), 'You're so small minded when you're at home, you just live in your own little world' and an Oakley housewife said 'When I was working I used to get a tremendous kick out of doing . . . housework. But now I'm doing it every day it really is the biggest bore of my life' (1976: 119).

Although Gershuny and Jones (1987) suggest that the amount of housework done by men has increased over the period 1961–1984, with a 10 per cent reduction in male paid work time accounted for mostly now in domestic labour, and a corresponding decrease in the amount of domestic work done by women in full- or part-time employment, it is still the case that far more housework is done by women than is by men. Certainly men are now more willing to help with tasks like hoovering, shopping, and washing up as well as doing DIY and other house-maintenance tasks, but few men regard housework as their responsibility. Housework then is work, it is time-consuming, and can be very exhausting, it leads to conflicts and contradictions as well as 'happy homes', and its nature cannot be understood without taking into account gender relations, because the sexual division of labour is still very embedded in housework.

Work in the community

Housework does not exhaust the category of unpaid work. A great deal of unpaid work is also done in the community on both a casual and on a more systematic basis, varying from giving surplus vegetables from an allotment to a neighbour, to doing Meals on Wheels or running a guide company. The extent to which work in the community is regarded as work is a moot point – in my research on women's leisure I found many women who saw their work in voluntary associations like the Women's Institute or fund-raising groups as part of their leisure and relaxation. Some voluntary organizations are very clearly leisure-oriented – hobby clubs like chess or flower-arranging or music clubs – but even these have to be organized and run by volunteers before the enjoyable parts can take place. But as Gershuny and Pahl (1985) point out, much community work often does things which would otherwise have to be paid for, whether it is care of the old or entertainment or a supply of garden produce. Finnegan (1985b) suggests that unpaid work in the community, whether for kin or acquaintances, is very important for developing and sustaining social networks. Voluntary organizations and caring work can provide services not provided by the state, as for example in the care of the elderly. Thus it is not the kind of work done which distinguishes community work from other forms but its unpaid nature and where it is carried out. Both men and women are involved in community work, although men are more likely to be members of formal organizations (Tomlinson 1979) and women more likely to do less organized work in the community. But many of the 'caring' voluntary groups are dominated by women, especially those in their forties and fifties.

Activity

Find out about unpaid work which takes place in your local area. Sources of information include neighbours, local news-

papers, and adverts in shop windows, as well as simply wandering about and doing some observing of what is happening. Try to find someone who does unpaid work for a voluntary organization – perhaps one you belong to yourself. Ask them about the work they do, why, and how long they've been doing it, and what they get out of it. How much time does it take up? Do they have any paid work as well? Is there still time for leisure or does the voluntary work take its place? If other students do similar interviews compare them to see what they tell you about unpaid work in the community.

Conclusion

What I have tried to explore in this chapter is some of the forms of work which exist outside the formal economy. These various forms divide into two groups – work with some kind of material reward in money or barter and unpaid work. Like work in the formal economy, work outside it is also influenced by class, race, and gender, by the state, and by power relations and ideologies. Work in the hidden economy is not necessarily more pleasant than a full-time job – sometimes it is the only form of paid work to be found, whilst in other cases it is simply another source of income or a preferred way of life. As with employment, some forms of unpaid work tend to have more status and better conditions than others – working to raise funds for the Rotary club versus cleaning the house for example. But furthermore, unpaid and paid work outside the formal economy have important consequences for leisure – in terms of time, money, energy, and enjoyment. I shall return to this theme in another chapter.

Further reading

On work in the hidden economy try Pahl (1984) Divisions of

Labour *(Blackwell), hard but with some interesting case studies. The classic book on housework is Oakley's (1976)* Housewife *(Penguin). On work in the community, S. Hatch's* Outside the State: Voluntary organisations in three English towns *(1980, Croom Helm) is worth a look or there is a certain amount in Pahl's book.*

4

Unemployment

In the last two chapters the focus has been on different forms of work, looking first at employment in the formal economy and then at other types of work, both paid and unpaid, in the hidden, domestic, and community economies. In this chapter I want to focus on those who are without formal employment of any kind; that is the unemployed. Now not everyone who is without formal employment is regarded or regards themselves as unemployed. It is an extremely difficult term to define and this is because many people and institutions have an interest in defining unemployment, including the state. Thus, official statistics on unemployment depend just as much on a particular definition as do sociological ones. (If you are interested in following up this point, see Slattery (1986) on official statistics.) For example in 1987 as I write this, the long-term unemployed are being encouraged to enter various schemes involving temporary work or training. If they do so, even though they are not thereby obtaining a permanent job nor necessarily getting any more money than they would on benefit, then they are no longer included in the statistics about the number of unemployed people. So we cannot rely on official figures either for a picture of who the unemployed are nor for a working definition, although clearly we have to use such statistics if we are to be able to say anything in general terms about the unemployed.

Nor is it very illuminating simply asking people if they are unemployed because even their reply is going to be somewhat dependent on the kind of image which unemployed people have at any given time. Gender and class differences also affect this self-definition. If there is a widespread belief, for instance, that male unemployment is caused by married women being in employment rather than at home, then there is a strong disincentive for married women without a job, even if they want one and are looking for employment, to describe themselves as housewives or mothers rather than unemployed, especially if they are ineligible for unemployment benefit. Equally there are those who to all intents and purposes are neither employed nor unemployed (e.g. those over official retiring age) but who will still take on a job if they can find one. As you saw from the previous chapter, work in the hidden economy, by its very nature, discourages people from talking about it, so that some of those without formal employment may nevertheless be making a living. Unemployment then is hard to pin down. The HMSO publication *Social Trends* uses the term 'economically inactive' to describe those who are *not* seeking paid employment. It includes the unemployed who *are* seeking work amongst those that it terms the 'economically active'. This is an interesting categorization, since the one obvious characteristic of the unemployed is their lack of economic activity, in the formal economy at any rate.

Changing pictures of unemployment

I am not going to attempt to give you masses of statistics about unemployment, partly because of the definitional problems already referred to but also because any set of statistics is soon out of date. Nevertheless since many of the researchers on unemployment hark back to the past (see for example Seabrook 1983) when unemployment was perceived to be as bad but when communities and people supposedly coped with it better, it may be useful to sketch a brief history.

The comparison that is often made at the present time is between the 1930s and the 1970s and 1980s, both periods of high unemployment but under very different sets of social and economic conditions. As Seabrook (1983) says, there are two common responses to the comparison. The first is that unemployment now is less humiliating than it was in the 1930s because state benefits prevent starvation now. The second reaction is that the present period is exactly like the 1930s and that nothing has been learnt at all from that last experience of mass unemployment. But in fact Seabrook and others suggest that things have changed, although not necessarily for the better; 'the decay of work and the changed function of the working class' (p. xiii) are two things which Seabrook picks out as differentiating the present time from the 1930s.

Marsden (1982) suggests that in the period since the 1960s, periodic rises in unemployment have led not to political protest (although clearly there has been some) but rather to 'complacency about levels of income support and . . . fears that state generosity is undermining the will to work' (p. 213). Yet the kinds of changes which have taken place in the formal economy (see Chapter 2 above) would suggest that some, even if short-term, rises in unemployment are likely as new technologies, products, and markets develop, some industries disappear, and others, demanding different skills, appear in their place. Also remember Pahl (1984) and the argument that the hidden economy may be in decline in the 1980s because the unemployed are more closely surveilled by both the community and the state. This in itself may discourage political action. If anything is undermining the will to work, it may be the lack of work rather than state benefits which is doing so.

The unemployment situation in Britain since the Second World War has undergone some significant changes. During the mid-1950s to mid-1960s, unemployment as measured in official statistics was very low (under 2 per cent of the adult population eligible for jobs) but it began to climb by the late 1960s, reaching 1 million in 1971 for the first time since before the war. Thereafter it continued to climb, so that by 1981 the total passed 2½ million, or one in ten of the workforce (Marsden 1982) and by mid-1985 it had reached 13.5 per cent (*Social Trends 1986*). Some of this rise in unemployment is due to changes in Britain's position in world trade, which in the period since 1945 has declined considerably. Sinfield (1981) suggests too that although unemployment in some other industrialized countries has also been rising, the situation in Britain is such that 'it cannot be simply a result of the international recession'.

Particularly affected by job losses have been manufacturing industries such as car production, steel, ship-building, and extraction industries like coal mining. The experiences of this process, sometimes known as deindustrialization, have not however been evenly felt across the country and by all social groups. Most affected have been the North East, Wales, Scotland, and the North West, and since 1979 the West Midlands. Deindustrialization has also affected inner-city areas much more than suburbs or small towns. Although the media often discuss the problems of unemployment as experienced by technical, professional, and managerial workers, Sinfield (1981) suggests that the discussions can be misleading. He contends that

> those most likely to be unemployed are people in low-paying and insecure jobs, the very young and the oldest in the labour force, people from ethnic minorities . . . people from among the disabled and handicapped, and generally those with the least skills and living in the most depressed

areas. Unemployment strikes . . . most harshly . . . those who are among the poorest and least powerful in the labour force and in society as a whole . . . the experience of being out of work may trap people at the bottom of society . . . most will go back into jobs as poorly or even more poorly paid.

(Sinfield 1981: 18–19)

Thus, as Marsden (1982) makes clear, many people are never unemployed, but those who are may well be in and out of employment all their lives. Very long-term unemployment over several years is not necessarily the typical experience of unemployment, although *Social Trends* for 1986 reported continuing faster growth in those out of work for over one year. A more typical experience of those groups particularly vulnerable to unemployment is what Seabrook (1983) describes as 'lengthening gaps between work, rather than continuous spells of being out of work' (p. 1).

This experience of being in a downward spiral of job loss followed by a further low-paid job, followed by another redundancy, is something which emerges strongly from almost all the recent studies of the unemployed, particularly those who live in high areas of high unemployment. Sinfield (1981) notes that a persistent criticism of the unemployed in depressed regions is that they will not move to find work. But the increasing north–south divide in Britain's job market is also reflected in things like the cost of living, availability of rented housing, and house prices, so moving may be very difficult. There are many personal and social costs to moving (compare the experiences of the car workers in the Chapter 2 case study). These costs may rise with age, and in many households there are the jobs of others to consider too. But in any case Sinfield points to the new towns as examples of how some people have moved to get jobs.

Activity

1 Find out about unemployment in your area; most local newspapers publish the area figures every so often, so keep an eye out for these or contact the newspaper office where you may be able to go through back issues; your nearest reference library may be able to help too. Another guide is how many jobs are advertised in job centres and in local papers; if there are almost none, this suggests employment isn't easy to come by, whereas if there are several pages then unemployment may be relatively low.

2 Try to discover what if any facilities are provided in your local area or nearest town for the unemployed. Is there a social or drop-in centre for them; what retraining possibilities are there? If you know anyone who is unemployed talk to them, provided they are willing to do so, about how they manage and what support they have had.

3 Find out what the current rate of unemployment benefit is – Post Offices, Citizens' Advice Bureaux, Money Advice Centres, and Welfare Rights bodies usually have leaflets giving these details. Remember there are different rates for different household situations like having lots of children as compared to one adult living alone. Then work out how much food and household essentials two adults and one child would need for one week – you could for instance price food essentials like tea, bread, milk, sugar, in a local shop – and how much these would cost. Don't forget things like rent, heating, clothes, shoes, household repairs, and cleaning.

The experiences of being unemployed

The young unemployed

Youth unemployment is not a problem confined to the last two decades in Western industrial societies, but since the

65

1970s in Britain and in other European countries, there have come to be increasing difficulties in finding employment for school leavers. There are many reasons for this: a reduction in the number of jobs available, particularly those requiring few or no skills, a growth in the number of areas of employment requiring not only technical skills, but also responsibility and autonomy which need time and experience to develop, the need to pay adult rates at younger ages, a decline in apprenticeships because of an equal decline in the traditional heavy and manufacturing industries with which these have often been associated, and increased competition between experienced adult workers and inexperienced young people for the same jobs. Governments have made many attempts to deal with youth unemployment: in Britain the Manpower Services Commission has increasingly turned its attention to youth unemployment, and the Youth Training Scheme for 16–17-year-olds leaving school has been extended to two years. In schools the MSC and other bodies have tried to develop ways of giving vocational training and positive attitudes towards industry and commerce, through things like the Technical and Vocational Educational Initiative (a scheme for 14–18-year-olds in schools and colleges) and the Certificate of Pre-Vocational Education for 16-year-olds who choose to stay on beyond the leaving age but don't want to take academic courses. But all the training in the world does not necessarily produce permanent jobs and for young people living in areas of high unemployment there can be severe social and personal difficulties.

The nature of these difficulties varies by gender, race, and class. But generally they include things like depression and feelings of listlessness and worthlessness (the 'real people have a job' syndrome), lack of money, social isolation, bitterness about the inability to get a job, and real difficulties in pursuing what are taken to be the 'normal' aspects of becoming an adult such as getting a place of one's own, marrying, having children, and so on. Not all young people fail to get a job when leaving school and never obtain one; as

Roberts, Duggan, and Noble (1981) found in their study of young unemployed in Manchester, Liverpool, London, and Wolverhampton, some drift in and out of jobs and others manage to hang on to a job for a year or more before becoming unemployed. Those who fared worst were those with no qualifications: 'even modest qualifications confer advantages, even in severely depressed labour markets. . . . Yet for any individual qualifications carry no guaranteed access to given levels of employment', say Roberts *et al.* (1981). Just as the adult labour market is segregated by gender, so is the youth job market, and in the Roberts study girls were more prone to unemployment than boys. Research on ethnic minority groups suggests they fare least well, especially if they are black (Troyna and Smith 1983).

Some unemployed young people are fairly heavily involved in the hidden economy, although the Roberts study found this was highest in London and that in other areas there was considerable competition for worthwhile casual work. The young unemployed lack the technical skills and contacts necessary to do well in casual work. Some turn to crime for money:

> 'There's a bit of work on the market but you can't rely on that. You can't keep asking your mum for money because she hasn't got much to spare. So you get into nicking because that's the only way to get a bit of money.'
>
> (Roberts *et al.* 1981: 23)

According to Griffin's (1985) study of working-class girls in Birmingham, unemployed females find the hidden economy harder to break into than boys; if they remain at home with their parents they may end up doing vast amounts of domestic labour and for some having a child presents the possibility of a worthwhile existence. Staying at home often produces tensions with parents, who may feel that not enough effort is put into looking for a job: 'my dad I can't really talk to, it's my mum, she's always at me to get a job. She doesn't understand that there are none, and it drives me mad' (Griffin 1985: 178).

The lack of a job also has quite a considerable impact on aspirations. Without a job it is difficult for young people to think themselves into the conventional moulds – breadwinning roles for men, motherhood and domestic work for women – even though their schooling will undoubtedly have led them to expect these kinds of traditional stereotyped roles. Both here and in the United States those studying young people in areas of high unemployment have found changes in the expectations of young people. Weiss (1987) found that in the city she studied in the USA, where there had been very heavy adult job losses in the steel industry, boys were beginning to appreciate the value of school and qualifications, but still saw themselves in the future as having a job and a stay-at-home wife/mother. But the girls did not want to get married for many years and preferred to set their sights on jobs alone.

Wallace (1986) in a study of the Isle of Sheppey found that aspirations to jobs and marriage expressed by school leavers were liable to collapse in the event of several years of unemployment or intermittent unemployment. An eighteen-year-old male said

> 'I want everything in life. I don't want to get married to a girl and 'ave nothing behind me . . . 'Cos it's no use getting married and you're on the dole . . . I'd sooner 'ave a job behind me, the money behind me, before I get married anyway.'

(Wallace 1986: 92)

Jobs that were unacceptable at 16 because of the low pay or the poor conditions came to be seen as better than nothing and whereas shortly after leaving school, not having a job was quite bearable as long as friends were in the same position, by age 21 the lack of a job was very serious; a girl who had left a series of factory jobs and then had a baby said her ideas had changed: 'Yes, I would do machining work now, and I would stick at it . . . I've got someone to look after now' (Wallace 1986: 103).

Female unemployment

For a long time studies of the adult unemployed virtually ignored women. It was assumed that women without employment 'chose' that situation and therefore found it easier to cope with than men. Even if their job loss was as a result of redundancy rather than pregnancy or marriage their alternative role in the household and family was considered ample compensation. More recently this view has been challenged by studies which suggest that women who lose their jobs suffer in many of the same ways as do men. There has also been a debate about whether women are more vulnerable to unemployment than men. It is certainly the case that their regional distribution has been different: in regions where there have been huge job losses from heavy industry, women have hung on to or obtained jobs in service industries. But elsewhere women have also suffered considerable job losses, as for example in the clothing and textile industries of Northern England.

The loss of a job by a woman is problematic no matter what her personal circumstances are. Income loss, decline in status, the absence of workmates, a drop in confidence, fewer leisure activities outside the home are all things found by Martin and Wallace (1984) in their study of women made redundant. The idea that women suffer less than men from unemployment because they have another role in the family did not appear to stand up. In most households women's earnings are as vital to the household budget as men's, even if dominant ideologies suggest it should be otherwise and if anything women set more store by friendships made at work than do men (Coyle 1984). What is different however is the reaction of women's households. Husbands with ambivalent attitudes towards their wives having jobs may be pleased if those jobs are lost. Martin and Wallace found evidence of many tensions in households for these kinds of reasons: 'He is pleased that I am now home full-time' (p. 244), although there were many husbands who regretted their wife's job loss because they were harder to live with or because of the effect on household income.

Like young people without jobs, unemployed women find that leisure is not easier to come by as a result: in Martin and Wallace's study many women complained of time on their hands, losing touch with friends, and being unable to continue former leisure pursuits. Women in Coyle's study who had lost their jobs in the textile industry found it harder, not easier, than before, to do their household chores. Many were prepared to take almost any other job they could get, even if the hours were longer and the pay poor. 'I would like a job . . . I hated it at the beginning. I was bored to tears. Every day I used to get fed up, but you get used to that boredom gradually. It's a way of life' (Coyle 1984: 77), said one woman. Some women did adjust to not having a job, especially if they had young children, although even then they looked forward to getting another job in the future. Women are less likely to spend their time whilst unemployed sitting idly around because most of them do have domestic responsibilities. But studies of unemployed men suggest that in the early stages of unemployment they too can find plenty of things to do. Most of the studies of unemployed women are too recent to know if like men they soon tire of work around the house and find themselves too depressed and lethargic to go out or use their time for leisure.

Unemployed men

Adult men have long been considered the group most likely to suffer the consequences of unemployment. Whilst the young school leaver may feel deprived of money and women who lose their jobs miss the money, work, and friendship, men who lose their jobs are seen to lose not only their identity, but their major role in life. The notion that men alone are household breadwinners has been challenged over the last decade by evidence (Martin and Roberts 1984) that women's jobs and incomes are also vital to household income. But the 'men as breadwinner' ideology lives on and whilst it exists men without employment do suffer considerably as a result. As with women who lose their jobs, men's reaction to their situation may change over time. Initially job loss is often cushioned by redundancy money, which may seem at first a huge sum of money:

'When I left work I had £1900 redundancy money; and with the few hundred I cashed from my pension scheme, it came to £2400. Even though you've no security later on, you feel you want to amass as much as you can at the time . . . it's more than most people have ever seen all at once in their whole lives. I think that dazzles people. You feel almost rich. But you're amazed at how soon it goes. . . . At first, great, you don't have to get up in the morning. . . . Then you have a twinge of anxiety . . . you have a casual look round, and the thing that strikes you is the shortage of work. You get more anxious; you see your money dwindle . . . then you find there's next to nothing in the bank.'
(unemployed telecommunications worker, Sunderland, quoted by Seabrook 1983: 113–14)

During the initial stages, men busy themselves with all kinds of projects – decorating, gardening, hobbies, and so on. Many of them even turn to housework, sometimes for the first time. They may see the time as a kind of holiday and certainly as a freedom from employment and fixed hours. Later on if no job appears they may begin to become depressed and to spend hours doing nothing but put their energies into looking for jobs. Their ideas about other jobs often tend to be quite idealistic at this stage – or at least they are concerned to get a job which is similar to their last in pay and so on. Later as unemployment becomes more prolonged they may begin to look for just any job. Leisure, unendingly, day after day, is no longer enjoyable and anyway most of it costs money:

'You don't realize, not until you've been out a couple of weeks. It costs money, decorating, and you can't keep it up.

71

Mostly it's just pottering. I get bored stiff. . . . Sometimes when you're working you wish you had a bit more time to do things, but I'd rather be working now and have no time. Sometimes I get to walking up and down with my hands in my pockets, walking up and down on the carpet. . . . A man *needs* work.'

(former skilled worker, quoted in Marsden 1982: 148–9)

The unemployed have endless time available to them but often derive little enjoyment from it; free time does not necessarily equal leisure.

The kinds of problems unemployed men suffer are for the most part little different from those experienced by other unemployed workers, but their vantage point is different. It is quite usual for young people and women to be seen about during the day, for example, students, housewives, mothers, but it is less usual for men. In our society having a job is a major part of masculine identity. Willis's (1977) 'lads' saw hard physical labour as something to look forward to after leaving the boredom of school. Without that job masculinity is more difficult to sustain. Men without jobs cannot be breadwinners, even if previously they were not the sole household earner anyway, and this strikes hard at identity, status, and friendships with other men, particularly if those men are still in employment. Unemployment puts a strain on sleep, money, health, and relationships. McKee and Bell (1984) found that unemployed men often resented wives who still had jobs. The men kept back personal spending money for themselves and refused to become involved in domestic work:

'I'd have the feeling as if people would be staring behind my back, my missus keeping me, she's paying for all the food, the clothes, the roof over our heads, paying for me to go out and have a drink. . . . If she just worked alone I'd probably go round the bend.'

(unemployed man quoted by McKee and Bell 1984: 19)

72

Even where men do start to do domestic work, women may resent the intrusion into what they regard as their sphere and put more pressure on their husbands to try to get some kind of job, whether in the formal or hidden economy. Both Burgoyne (1985) and McKee and Bell (1984) have evidence to suggest that marriages are often severely threatened by male unemployment. That threat is not only because of material deprivations but also because of the effects of prevalent ideas about male–female relationships and male identity in our society.

Ethnic minority unemployment

There is general agreement that ethnic minority groups, especially those who are black and working-class, are more likely to experience unemployment than those with similar qualifications or job experience who are white (see current issue of *Social Trends* for up-to-date unemployment figures comparing ethnic minority groups to others). Smith (1981) found that the process of seeking a job was made much harder by discrimination. He describes research which involved getting black and white applicants to apply for the same jobs and comparing the responses they got on the same day. There may also be indirect discrimination: Wrench and Lee (1983) studying the employment prospects of young blacks in Birmingham found that many firms preferred to take on local youngsters so that they would be punctual. As there were almost no factories in areas like Handsworth where many black unemployed school leavers lived, they had little chance of employment on such a basis. Of course many of the things which affect all unemployed people – poverty, boredom, lack of status, too much time on their hands, marriage break-up, loss of friends, and so on – also apply to those from ethnic minority groups. But in addition they have to face prejudice, discrimination, poor housing, and many other disadvantages arising from racism. The 1984 Policy Studies Institute Report found that racialism and direct discrimination were continuing to have an effect on the lives of black people in Britain, including violence and other forms of harassment. An eighteen-year-old Afro-Caribbean told Seabrook (1983)

'My parents came here in the 1950s. They didn't mind doing rough jobs. My Dad worked in a hospital, a porter, and my mother was in a plastics factory. My Dad was sick and he lost his job and he went on invalidity benefit. My Mum was made redundant. You go to school . . . Then you get a bit older, you find you haven't learnt anything, you can't even do the exams. . . . So that's one big lost illusion for your parents. The next thing, there's not even the jobs they come here to do. Nothing. . . . That's the next big disappointment. . . . Then, you can't go anywhere but you're stopped by the police . . . you're accused of nicking, . . . they take you down the station, you get roughed about. So that's the end . . . your parents . . . lose hope. They realize no black people is going to get anywhere because they're black.'

(Seabrook 1983: 65–6)

Activity

Imagine you have lost your job and have got £2000 redundancy money; what problems do you think you will face in the first two months after losing your job and how would you deal with them? If no job comes along after six months how would you spend your time and what would you do? Do you think leisure would still be important to you? Would you try to get involved in the hidden economy or community work? What about domestic work? If other students do this activity too you might find it useful to compare your accounts.

Conclusion

This brief discussion about unemployment will, I hope, have given you some issues to think about in relation to leisure and work as well as an insight into what lives without employment are like. Unemployment is often welcomed initially because it is seen as a rest or a holiday; leisure, the hidden economy, household tasks all get accomplished. But gradually these slip, boredom and apathy set in, and hours may be spent just sitting or staying in bed. Unemployment doesn't just affect people through loss of income, but also through loss of identity and their aspirations. The work ethic is still very much with us, however much people (usually those still in well-paid employment) may talk about a leisured society and how desirable that is. But even in unemployment, social divisions are still important – age, gender, race, and class shape the particular experiences of unemployment that individuals face. There is also little sign in the studies of the unemployed that any alternative economy, hidden, domestic, or whatever, can replace formal employment. I shall return to this issue in the final chapter.

Further reading

Two useful books which cover a wide range of issues to do with unemployment are A. Sinfield (1981) What Unemployment Means *(Martin Robertson) and J. Seabrook (1983)* Unemployment *(Paladin). Sinfield is a more academic book, whilst Seabrook documents many people's views and experiences during a round England trip. If you are especially interested in women's unemployment the best and most readable book is Angela Coyle's* Redundant Women *(1984, Women's Press).*

5

Leisure

What is leisure?

In this chapter the focus will be on leisure, a concept which, as you will by now have realized, is, along with work and unemployment, a term with a number of possible definitions, and which is far from being easy to apply to concrete individuals and their actions. One reason why leisure is a difficult concept to define firmly, as we saw in Chapter 1, is precisely because of the close links between work, leisure, and unemployment, especially once we move away from regarding work as just paid employment. Thus, for a woman or man in a 9am to 5pm job and with no household responsibilities, leisure might be activities and interests occurring outside the hours of paid work – dancing, watching TV, holidays, going to the pub, walking, or playing pool. If you are the parent of a very young child some of these activities would be more difficult to carry out – even watching TV becomes less enjoyable if it is constantly interrupted. Or the activity might take a different form, such as walking with a baby buggy round the park rather than going for a ten-mile walk in the hills. For those outside of formal employment many leisure activities might prove too expensive: the pub, dancing, holidays are a few examples. Other activities this group do could become ways of filling time rather than being enjoyable ways to relax: walking aimlessly round the streets or watching TV all day because it's cheap, but without really wanting to watch anything in particular. For some people whose work is mainly in the informal economy, going to the pub or playing pool might be a way of developing contacts which lead to casual work rather than a way of recuperating after employment is over for the day. Historically, as we saw in Chapter 1, paid employment and leisure have been heavily interconnected in industrial societies, with (mostly male) workers struggling to gain leisure time from their employers. But more recent research has suggested that leisure is also something that people outside formal employment struggle over – housewives for example – and there is nothing like rising unemployment rates for bringing about a rash of books and articles about 'the leisure society' and 'has work a future?'.

Activity

In Chapter 3 one of the suggested activities included asking you to keep a detailed diary for two days and then trying to decide which of the things you wrote down were work and which not. If you did this activity you might find it worthwhile to go back to your notes about it and look at which things you thought were leisure. If you did not have the time to do the activity when you read that chapter, you might want to try it now. It would certainly be helpful here. There was also an activity in Chapter 1 which involved asking someone else to say how in their own lives they distinguished between work and leisure and this too would be worth glancing at again.

One of the reasons that studying and particularly researching leisure is difficult is that whilst there are obviously many social influences which shape its form, the *experience* and *meaning* of leisure are intensely personal to a given individual. So, for example, a busy single person with a demanding job and hectic social life might regard their social life and being with lots of other people in commercial leisure locations as essential to their existence as well as being enjoyable and relaxing. An unemployed teenager, on the other hand, may dislike going to places like pubs or discos, not only because it involves spending scarce money, but also because it forces contact with people who do have jobs and reminds them of their own jobless state. An overworked housewife at home with children may regard half an hour on her own at home, whilst her husband takes the children to the park, as far more relaxing than going to the pub on a Sunday with her children.

The *context* in which activities occur is also important and closely linked to the meanings which people attribute to their leisure. Thus the same activity done by the same person in different contexts may have entirely different meanings – hence drinking alcohol may be a part of work when it is done as a means to ease the tension of meeting business colleagues, relaxation when taken as part of a meal with friends in a restaurant, and a social obligation when it consists of drinking cooking sherry as part of a duty visit to an elderly aunt. Cooking a meal at home when time is short and hungry children keep asking when it will be ready may be classed as work whilst organizing a barbecue on holiday for the same children may be an enjoyable activity.

Leisure is often a form of *activity*, but not necessarily particular kinds of activities. Thus playing football or tennis can equally be categorized differently by various people: a professional player would regard it as a job, a Saturday afternoon player think of it as leisure, and a schoolchild who dislikes compulsory school sport might consider it a form of torture. So leisure cannot simply be equated with certain types of activities. Nor is it necessarily a hobby, like stamp collecting, flower arranging or researching family history. Nevertheless, leisure often involves *consuming* things, whether it is goods like sports clothing and video recorders or services like leisure centres and bingo clubs.

Time clearly enters into the definition – since leisure is frequently regarded as 'time off'. But not everyone does the kind of work which provides unambiguous free time and some people combine their work and leisure together. Ironing whilst watching TV represents both work and leisure for a housewife, but also shows how much more difficult leisure is when the work done is not neatly parcelled up into tasks and time slots. Parker (1983) also uses the example of residential social workers as a group who find it difficult to entangle their work and leisure because they live and work in the same place and their leisure often involves the clients whom they care for. The unemployed have a lot of free time, but, as the last chapter showed, the very abundance of time may make it hard for its use and availability to be considered pleasurable.

Choice is another aspect of leisure, so that one defining characteristic could be things which an individual chooses to do (going out for a meal, watching a video, meeting friends), rather than those she or he is obliged to do (like their job or household responsibilities). But there are few people who have a completely free choice of leisure interests and activities – life is just not like that! Our education, income, time, household responsibilities, age, health, jobs, and social relationships all affect what leisure we have and what we 'choose' to do in it; so too does the type of society we live in as well as class, gender, and ethnicity. Fear of attack and racial or sexual harassment can, for example, severely limit the out-of-home leisure of women and black people.

Roberts (1981) suggests that we can group all the various definitions of leisure under two headings, the first of which is leisure as part of a way of life, which would include the use of time and the ways in which leisure relates to and flows into and out of other aspects of our lives like jobs, caring for children, and decorating the house. In this sense, says Roberts, leisure is basically *'spare* or *free time* in which we can please ourselves; the part of life that remains when we have fulfilled our duties' (Roberts 1981: 9–10). The second heading he sees as a type of activity characterized by something called 'play' or recreation, separated from the rest of life by different rules, places, and times: 'play involves stepping outside our normal routines, and our normal "selves". It enables us to express and develop aspects of our characters that would otherwise remain hidden' (Roberts 1981: 10). Play, then, is something which is meaningful and enjoyable in itself and which expresses our own identity and personality. So this category would include choice, consumerism, meaning, and context. The difficulty with these two headings lies in the fact that neither is exclusive of the other – play is a part of our lives and time, meaning, context, and choice affect both of these. Also, neither really tackles the question of who sees themselves as having a right to leisure, something which affects choice, consuming, and meaning, way of life, and play. As we saw in the last chapter on unemployment, the unemployed have plenty of time but without the stimulus of paid work may not see leisure as something to which they are entitled. It is extremely difficult to understand leisure unless it is treated as part of our life styles as a whole, just as it is impossible to understand the significance of jobs, the informal economy and unemployment unless they are seen in the context of our lives as a whole. This, along with the personal meaningful aspects of leisure, means that leisure itself is not always easy to study and research. It is certainly a good deal harder to study than paid employment.

Socially visible leisure

A great deal of the sociological research on leisure has been on what might be termed 'socially visible' leisure, that is activities which are relatively easily seen and measured or otherwise studied, rather than things which are hidden from view by their location or because people want to protect their privacy. Hence we know a good deal more about who visits stately homes or where people go on holiday than we know about sex as a leisure activity or about leisure in the home in general. There are aspects of leisure, for example friendship, and struggles in households over who has leisure time, about which we know very little indeed. Sociological research, especially that involving surveys, is nearly always greater in extent when it deals with phenomena which are easily visible and not too difficult to research; there is also a tendency for research to reflect the concerns and activities of those groups who are themselves highly visible in society – men rather than women, ethnic majorities rather than ethnic minorities. We can nevertheless learn a good deal about people's leisure from surveys and other large-scale research, even though the difficulties of researching leisure have sometimes meant that certain aspects of that leisure are missed out altogether.

The use of time

One way of trying to overcome the concentration on easily visible leisure has been to explore leisure through the use of time by individuals. A number of studies have focused on the relationship between time spent on leisure and time spent on other activities, partly because there is an underlying belief that in Britain between the 1960s and the 1980s the amount of time people have for leisure has gone up. This belief is based on factors like the shorter hours of employment worked by those in full-time jobs; from an average of 40 basic hours per week in the 1960s (this figure excludes overtime) to 36.5 basic hours for women and 38.2 hours for men in full-time employment (*Social Trends 1987*). Holiday entitlement has also gone up over the same period: *Social Trends* notes that whilst in 1963, 97 per cent of full-time manual workers were only entitled to two weeks annually, by 1985, 99 per cent of the same category of workers had a basic entitlement of four weeks or more. Of course this is far from a complete picture; it tells us nothing about those who are not in full-time paid employment and hides the fact that male British workers, in addition to their basic working hours, have the highest levels of overtime of all the EEC countries. It also assumes that hours free from paid employment are available for leisure, although we know that many other things, including household duties and sleep, must be fitted into those time periods. Some researchers (e.g. Szalai 1972, who compared the use of time by people in several countries) have tried to discover how much time is spent on different kinds of activities and obligations by different groups of people. This has been done mainly through the use of time budget studies, which are really a development of the kind of diary keeping suggested on p. 43. The Henley Centre for Forecasting has attempted to blend together the available information on use of time to discover how employment status, age, and gender affect the amounts of time spent on different things, including jobs, household work, sleep, and other essential tasks.

Activity

Use the table below to answer the following questions:
1 Who spends the most time each week in employment? And who least?
2 Which group devotes most time to essential activities?
3 Who spends most time in employment, travel, and essential activities?
4 Who has most free time?
5 What significance does gender have in the distribution of time to different activities (you might find it helpful to refer

back to Chapter 3 to remind yourself about what happens
in households)?
6 Are any groups left out of the statistics? If so which? Why
do you think they are left out?
7 How reliable do you think the information in the table is?
Why might it not be totally accurate?
8 What does the table tell us about the time available for
leisure for the groups mentioned? What sorts of factors,
from the table, seem to influence the availability of free
time?

Leisure outside the home

Although Table 1 tells us some fascinating things about the

Table 1 *Time use in a typical week – Great Britain 1985*

| | Full-time employees | | Part-time employees | | | |
	Males	Females	Males	Females	Housewives	Retired people
weekly hrs spent on:						
Employ-ment and travel	45.0	40.8	24.3	22.2		
Essential activities	33.1	45.1	48.8	61.3	76.6	49.8
Sleep	56.4	57.5	56.6	57.0	59.2	60.2
Free time weekdays	2.6	2.1	4.5	3.1	4.2	7.9
Free time weekends	10.2	7.2	7.8	5.9	5.6	9.1

Source: Table 10.1, *Social Trends* 1987: 163, taken from *Leisure Futures*, Summer
1986, the Henley Centre for Forecasting.
Notes: Travel means travel to and from place of employment. Essential activities
means cooking, shopping, childcare, eating meals, washing, getting up, and
going to bed.

different ways in which employed, unpaid, and retired workers of both sexes spend their time, it has limitations. It does not tell us what the so-called free time is used for. There is no information on class or ethnicity; nor, apart from the reference to retired people, does it tell us about age or life-course differences. Neither does it give us any clues about the quality of the time available for leisure (an hour in a quiet restaurant may be of higher quality than three hours spent at home with a crying baby whilst trying to read a book). It does not deal with dual use of time, for work *and* leisure.

The General Household Survey is a useful starting point for looking at what people actually do in their leisure time. It is based on detailed interviews with a national sample of the UK population, although the questions asked about leisure are not totally reliable because they ask about leisure in the four weeks prior to interview (so the time of year is influential – gardening is more likely to be done in summer, TV watched in winter) and because the questions ask people to choose from a list of preselected activities. Nevertheless, the data are helpful and give some broad indications about different patterns of leisure. What they cannot do is to indicate the ease or difficulty with which people pursue their out-of-home leisure, the constraints and struggles which influence what is seen as possible as well as actually done. What is most interesting about the figures in Table 2 is that they suggest that men and women broadly do similar social and cultural activities. There is one very significant difference: far fewer women go out for a drink than do men. There are a few minor differences on seaside outings, cinema, theatre visits, leisure classes, visits to fairs, and dancing, all of which are done slightly more by women. Indeed other studies suggest that social and cultural activities appear to be done much more by women than by men (Deem 1986, Green, Hebron, and Woodward 1987). Women are much more likely to be engaged in artistic activities and to belong to a whole range of voluntary groups too, from the Women's Institute to fund-raising organizations, although male club membership is higher because this includes drinking and sports clubs (Deem 1986, Tomlinson 1979). Adult education, which includes rather more than the 'leisure classes' mentioned in the table, is also dominated by women (Thompson 1983). Many factors are left out of Table 2, with age, ethnicity, life course, income, and occupational status being just some of the omissions. There is nothing on young people's leisure, which often revolves around things which don't cost much, such as going to pubs, but may also include things done much less by older people – discos, youth clubs, hanging round town centres and shopping centres, and so on.

Table 2 *Social and cultural activities of men and women, U.K., 1983*

% in each group participating in last 4 weeks:	men	women
Open air outings		
Seaside	7	8
Country	3	3
Parks	3	4
Entertainment, social, and cultural activities		
Cinema	7	8
Visiting historical buildings	8	8
Theatre/opera/ballet	4	5
Museums/art galleries	3	3
Amateur music/drama	3	3
Leisure classes	1	2
Fairs/amusement arcades	1	2
Going out for meal	41	40
Going out for drink	64	46
Dancing	10	12
Sample size (100% numbers)	8,751	10,319

Source: General Household Survey 1983, from *Social Trends 1985*: 149, Table 10.3.

The table also does not tell us with whom the activities were undertaken – were more women accompanied by children when going to the seaside and fairs, for example, which might account for the higher figures? Do men go more to the pub with other men, as Smith's (1987) much more detailed analysis of the General Household Survey data suggests? The other striking thing about this table is that the only very frequently done activities by anyone are going out for a meal and going for a drink. You need to realize in this connection that going out for a meal might mean going to the house of a friend or relative as well as to a café or restaurant. Going out for a drink similarly covers a wide range – from a smart night club or wine bar to a working men's club. The table also misses out two other important aspects of out-of-home leisure – sport and holidays – as well as telling us little about activities such as bingo and betting. *Social Trends* (1987) tells us that both bingo and betting have declined over the last decade, although activities involving casinos and gaming machines have increased. Bingo is dominated by working-class women, attracted not so much by the gambling aspect, which is very small, but by the cheapness, comparative safety, and security of bingo halls compared to pubs, clubs, and other leisure venues, and the opportunity to get out of the house and meet other women (Dixey and Talbot 1984). Men predominate in betting, casinos, and the use of gaming machines.

Sport

Involvement in sport is another fairly visible leisure activity, although sport as leisure can mean several different things. It can refer to *active participation*, which tends to decline with age and which is not particularly high in Britain anyway, compared to other European countries. Or it can mean *spectating*, either in person or through television and video watching. For women in particular, there is also often a third level, *helping to support those who play sport* whether through secretarial services, washing kit or preparing refreshments. This third level is extremely unlikely to be picked up in official surveys, which are best at dealing with active and spectator sport. The General Household Survey suggests that so far as active sports participation is concerned, walking is the most popular for all adults, with 19 per cent of men and 17 per cent of women having been on a walk of at least 2 miles in the previous two weeks prior to being interviewed in 1983. For women the next most popular sport was swimming, followed by keep fit and yoga, whilst billiards, snooker, and darts were popular with men, with football, fishing, golf, and squash some way behind. Men, according to these data, participate much more in sport than women and women's participation exceeded that of men only in yoga, keep fit, and horse riding. The GHS data in this form do not tell us about ethnicity, age, or income levels, nor about whether sport is something which people tend to engage in with friends, partners, or children. Other evidence suggests that there are big class differences in the kinds of sport done (Roberts 1981) – darts, for instance, tends to be working-class whilst horse riding is usually done by the middle-classes – and that women, in so far as they do sport, are more likely to be accompanied by children, which may explain the popularity of walking and swimming (Deem 1986, Green, Hebron, and Woodward 1987). Furthermore, active sport is a leisure activity which has a distinctly masculine image; as one woman said in my own research when I asked her about sport, 'that's what men do isn't it?' (Deem 1986: 68). So far as spectator sport is concerned, football and motor sports were the most popular in 1985, followed by greyhound racing, horse racing, and Rugby League, with men being the principal spectators (*Social Trends* 1987). Although football far outweighs any other spectator sport in popularity, it is nevertheless in serious decline (Roberts 1981).

We tend to think of being involved in sport as something positive, with a number of benefits ranging from enjoyment gained through spectating to fitness obtained through regular sports participation. Some theorists point out how closely bound up sport is with the needs of industrial production, with the emphasis on consuming goods and services (Clarke and Critcher 1985). But there are other less pleasant aspects of sport, like soccer hooliganism (Roberts 1981). And not everyone who engages in sport necessarily does it willingly. Scraton (1987) describes how teenage schoolgirls are often very resistant to compulsory physical education at school; nor is this resistance to sport at school confined to girls. But on the whole, boys are more likely to be involved in sport throughout their teens than are girls. However, this greater young male enthusiasm for sport can present other problems and issues. Carrington and Leaman (1983) point out that whilst access to sport is being improved for groups like the young unemployed, often through special schemes and concessionary rates of payment, this may also mean that it is being used to control those groups by keeping them off the streets and that money is spent on this rather than on, say, providing more jobs for the unemployed.

Holidays

Holidays are the third major aspect of socially visible leisure. The total number of holidays taken by people resident in Britain has risen considerably since 1971 when 41 million holidays were taken (7 million of these abroad). In 1985 49 million holidays were taken, with 16 million of these being abroad. The latter are mostly to Europe, with Spain remaining the favourite holiday destination in 1985 with over half of foreign holidays involving staying in hotels, although hotel-based holidays abroad are decreasing, with an increase in the numbers using rented apartments and accommodation as paying guests. Since we have already seen that the paid holiday entitlement of full-time employees has also been going up over this period, the increase in the total number of holidays is not surprising. However, holiday statistics are worth a close scrutiny. We tend to assume that holidays are very enjoyable and relaxing for all concerned, although those of you who have ever been an unwilling member of a family holiday may realize otherwise. As Tysoe (1985) notes, holidays, whilst sometimes intended to improve family relationships, often make tensions and conflicts worse, because people who are not normally together all day long are suddenly placed in close proximity to each other. Research on women's leisure suggests that women may get a particularly raw deal on self-catering holidays if they are still expected to do all the household chores for the rest of the family (Deem 1986). Of course not everyone goes on family holidays anyway; indeed one reason for going on holiday, especially for the young, the single, and the elderly, is to meet new people; also often important are a change of scene, warm weather, and new activities. Many holidays are undoubtedly relaxing and help people recuperate from the strains of work and everyday life. But not everyone can afford holidays, and time off from employment isn't always spent in going away – it may instead be used to catch up on housework, visit relatives, or to do home decorating and repairs. Those elderly people on very low incomes, people who are handicapped, the unemployed, and working-class single parents are all groups who are much less likely than others to go away on holiday, even though some of them have a great deal of so-called free time.

Leisure spending

Much visible leisure, like holidays or spectator sport or visiting the cinema, does involve spending money and consuming things, which is why class and income are important factors influencing leisure. The most reliable national statistics on leisure expenditure come from the Family Expenditure Survey, based like the General Household Survey on a representative national sample. This evidence (reported in *Social Trends* 1987) suggests that in 1985, households (remember that a household doesn't necessarily mean a nuclear family with two adults and dependent children, but can mean adult only households, or households of people who are not blood relations) spent an average of £25.98 per week on leisure. The highest proportion of this was on alcoholic drink (22 per cent of weekly spending) which fits well with the evidence of Table 2, where we saw that going out for a drink was by far the most frequently done leisure activity for both sexes. The next largest areas of spending were on holidays, television, radio, and musical instruments (you might pause to think why these last three are lumped together, given that television is much the most popular of the three but costs little other than the annual licence fee once a set is purchased, that listening to the radio costs next to nothing, and that relatively few adults actually play a musical instrument), followed by eating out and books, newspapers, and magazines. What doesn't appear in these figures at all, possibly as a consequence of the categories used, is expenditure on microelectronic goods for leisure, especially home computers and electronic games, which are a rapidly increasing sector of leisure spending, especially for males of all ages. As you would expect, households where at least one adult was in employment spent more on leisure and a higher proportion of their total household spending, than retired pensioner households or those where there was unemployment.

Leisure at home

Looking at spending on leisure starts you thinking about leisure at home as well as leisure outside the home. Not all the money spent on leisure appears in estimates of leisure spending; so, for instance, cars are used for both work and leisure, as is money spent on renting or buying a home. Of course leisure does not always involve expenditure. But leisure which does, tends to be much more visible. Leisure in the home covers a very wide range of things, some of which are hidden and others (like owning a TV or reading a newspaper) which are well known about. It may also be something which is more common to certain groups than to others — women of all ages are more likely to have home-based leisure, from adolescents to adult women.

Activity

1 Try to make a list of the things you and your friends do at home which might be classed as leisure (go back to the beginning of the chapter if you want to remind yourself about ways to decide what leisure is). Use two columns in the list, one for things which cost money and another for ones which don't (or very little, like TV).
2 Which of the things on the list do you think it would be easy for a researcher to find out about, either by giving you a questionnaire or interview or through visiting your home or through looking at statistical evidence? Which would be more difficult to find out about, and why? Are there some things you didn't write down which might be classed as leisure using the criteria suggested at the beginning of this chapter?
3 If you are female, think what else your list might include and what is on your list that might not be there if you were male. If you are male, what might a female include and exclude?
4 If you were interested in studying leisure at home, how do you think you would go about it (you might want to consult McNeill's *Research Methods* (1985) in this series to help you with this)? What problems do you think you might encounter? Do you think people would resent, enjoy, or not be bothered about research into their leisure?

Once again the General Household Survey is a useful starting point for finding out about leisure in the home, although it does not help us very much in so far as the leisure of teenagers is concerned; if you are under 21 yourself, when was the last time you did any gardening (except under duress!) or needlework or house repairs? The 1983 Survey suggests that in the four weeks before they were interviewed, 65 per cent of men had listened to tapes or records, 51 per cent had done house repairs or DIY, 50 per cent had read a book, and the same percentage had done some gardening. 62 per cent of women had listened to records or tapes, 61 per cent had read a book, 48 per cent had done some needlework or knitting, and 39 per cent had done some gardening. *Social Trends* (1987) indicates that most adults spend a good deal of time watching TV – in the first quarter of 1986 (remember this was winter) women had spent an average of 30 hours 38 minutes per week on TV viewing and men were only a little way behind with an average of 26 hours 4 minutes – but much less time listening to the radio, with an average in 1985 of 8 hours 40 minutes per person per week. Men are much more likely to read newspapers than women; women's choice of reading matter is more likely to be a book or magazine (*Social Trends* 1985). But just taking this information at face value does not in itself tell us why people do the particular activities they do. Nor does it provide a complete picture; the missing information on the under-21s has already been mentioned, but there is also no indication of the by now widespread use of home computers for leisure. Nor do the data tell us whether leisure is the only motivating factor for the particular activities undertaken (this is a drawback with all large-scale survey research: it tells us about *what* but rarely *why*). As Roberts (1981) points out, people who watch TV may be doing so for a variety of reasons – to relax during a favourite soap opera or concert, to give them something else to do whilst looking after their children, or because they are taking an Open University course. During my own leisure research on women, a lot of mothers said that they gained a great deal of enjoyment and pleasure from their children, yet children never appear in lists of leisure activities and interests and can be hard work much of the time too (Deem 1986).

Women's leisure is much more likely to take place in the

home than men's, especially during weekdays and evenings during the week (Deem 1986, Green, Hebron, and Woodward 1987). This is only partly because women, especially those with significant household and childcare responsibilities, are less likely to be in full-time employment; this in itself potentially provides more time for leisure, although it also means women have less money of their own (sometimes none if they are not in paid work at all). But the nature of women's childcare and household commitments means it is often more difficult for women to go out than it is for men. Also women often have to negotiate hard with male partners if they wish to go out, especially on weekday evenings or if they want to go out alone or with other women (Green, Hebron, and Woodward 1987). In the home itself, the quality of time and leisure experienced by many women is often affected by the unstructured, unspecific demands of housework and caring for the rest of the household; leisure for the rest of the household can mean more work for women (getting drinks and snacks, keeping children amused whilst Dad watches his favourite TV programme, washing and ironing clothes). Women's at-home leisure then is frequently interrupted by their unpaid work and their leisure often combined with that work: listening to the radio whilst cooking a meal, a talk with a friend whilst supervising children's play. My own research on women's leisure in Milton Keynes (Deem 1986) and an intensive study of Sheffield women by Green, Hebron, and Woodward (1987) found that as well as TV, knitting, and other crafts, reading and gardening done by women at home, sitting down, and 'doing nothing' were extremely popular. Griffin (1985) has noted that even very young women in particular circumstances may spend a lot of leisure time at home, sometimes with their friends too, as compared to young men.

It is worth noting that apart from a study of leisure in the home involving both men and women (Glyptis and Chambers 1982) there have been no UK studies of men's leisure at home, except as part of research like Pahl (1984) whose main

93

concerns were wider issues. You might want to think about why such research has not been done, when men's out-of-home leisure has been extensively studied, particularly in relation to sport. Of course, men are not exclusively engaged in leisure when they are at home; they also work at home, as we saw in the chapter on the informal economy. They are particularly likely to be doing tasks like car repairs, home repairs, and DIY, which the General Household Survey classes as leisure but which may often be a necessity, even if also sometimes enjoyable. Indeed Gershuny and Jones (1987) argue that men's involvement in domestic work as a whole, including cooking and washing up, childcare, and shopping, has doubled since the mid-1970s with a corresponding decline in women's involvement, although they do point out that since in 1974–5 men were only doing a tiny proportion of housework, they still have a lot of ground to make up. However, Gershuny and Jones also note, as did Oakley in her study of housework (1974), that the time devoted to childcare by households over the period 1974/5–1983/4 has gone up. This has involved both men and women, surprisingly at a period when the birthrate has been at best static, and so there have statistically been fewer children per household to care for. Nevertheless, although men do work at home, they still currently do a lot less of the routine tasks than women. The Milton Keynes and Sheffield studies suggest women find it more difficult to take time off for leisure at home than men and are less likely than men to think of themselves as having a right to leisure. The home is much more a workplace for most women than it is for men, unless men belong to a minority who do paid work from home, and the context in which women's at-home leisure takes place is thus less satisfactory than for the majority of men for whom home is a place where they go to relax.

Influences on and views about leisure

Much of this chapter has been devoted to exploring patterns

of leisure and leisure time use. Although some time was spent at the beginning considering definitions of leisure and although during the examination of leisure patterns some references have been made to some of the factors influencing who does what, where, and when, no systematic attempt has been made to explain this. Explaining leisure is a complicated sociological exercise to which there are at present few satisfactory answers. It is interesting that the classical sociological perspectives, whilst concerned to explain why people do certain jobs or have particular religious or political beliefs, have almost nothing to say about leisure. Certainly it is clear that factors like education, age, class and income, car ownership, gender, and ethnicity are all key factors in leisure, with middle-class graduates who have reasonable incomes and their own cars being particularly likely to have high rates of leisure participation.

There are actually few very clear divides which can determine or tell us who is likely to do what kind of leisure (Roberts 1981). But I disagree with Roberts' view that class is not a major divide: it influences way of life, life style, income, occupation, and the values and beliefs people have, and so is bound to affect leisure and leisure experiences. So too gender is of fundamental importance to leisure, even to the extent of cutting across class boundaries. The Sheffield study (Green, Hebron, and Woodward 1987) found that women from all social groups shared common fears about going into the city centre at night alone or with other women; the necessity to negotiate and argue for leisure time and space was similarly not confined to working-class women and their partners. The importance of gender is related to the power relations which exist between the sexes and the effects this has on who does what paid and unpaid work, who has what leisure, and who has what rights to leisure. Ethnicity too may have quite a significant impact on leisure, although few researchers have so far bothered to consider this angle.

Work itself is an important, but not absolute, influence on leisure: people in the same kind of work don't necessarily have the same leisure interests, nor is it the case that long hours of work always preclude leisure, although shift work for example can disrupt leisure and normal patterns of sociability. The availability of time does not in itself help to explain who has what leisure because the unemployed and the elderly, both of whom have time in abundance, often have very little leisure. Age and stage in the life course are important in explaining participation in some activities, particularly sport. The young often have little money but go out a good deal, especially if they are male. People with young children are often confined to at-home leisure unless they also take their children. But those in their forties and fifties are often as active in out-of-home leisure as teenagers, albeit in different pursuits. For those over retirement age, leisure becomes more possible but ill-health and lack of money and transport may reduce their involvement; it is apparent, for instance, that some retired people who decide to go and live at the seaside have a miserable time rather than a leisure-filled life (Karn 1977). Income is helpful if someone wants to take up an expensive activity – show jumping or collecting antiques – but some individuals with very low incomes have as many or more leisure interests as those with high incomes. Owning a car helps if you want to be involved in leisure which doesn't take place at home or very close to it but not all non-car drivers are bereft of out-of-home leisure. Some of the most useful studies we have of leisure have been those which do study it as part of a way of life – Clarke, Critcher, and Johnson's (1979) *Working Class Culture*, Griffin's (1985) study of female working-class school leavers, Pahl's (1984) study of the informal economy on the Isle of Sheppey, Dixey and Talbot's (1982) study of bingo in Leeds, Edgell's (1980) research on the lives of middle-class couples, Yeandle's (1984) study of the lives of women with jobs and children – because they can at least begin to untangle the complex questions about who, why, and what.

Activity

1 Try to find out what leisure activities and organizations there are in your area. Good sources of information apart from your own friends and family are local papers and noticeboards in public libraries. Do there seem to be a lot of things on offer or very few (this is likely to be affected by where you live – a village will have less, in general, than a large city) and do the things available seem to appeal to particular groups (the young, those with cars, the elderly)? Do you need transport or a lot of money to do many of the things? What provision is there for the unemployed, for women at home with children, for people who are disabled, for ethnic minority groups? Are there more private providers than local authority ones?

2 Take any one leisure activity, maybe one you are yourself involved in, or one done by someone you know. Try to find out what sort of people do it, and why; whether it is popular or a minority interest; how much time and money it requires; whether some groups of people are excluded from doing it. If others in your teaching group do this as well it might be useful to compare your findings.

3 Get hold of and read one of the studies mentioned in the last paragraph of the chapter before the activity. (Look up Clarke, Critcher, and Johnson 1979; Pahl 1984; Dixey and Talbot 1982; Edgell 1980; Yeandle 1984, in the references.) If you can't find any of those mentioned see if you can find a similar study – perhaps one on a particular community. What does it tell you about the why, who, and what of leisure? What does it miss out? How do the authors explain the lives and life styles of the individuals about whom they are writing?

Leisure and the state

The state and industry and commerce are important sources of ideas about leisure and of the actual services and goods used for leisure, just as they are crucial in defining ideas about as well as the structure of paid and unpaid work and unemployment. Legislation like the Ten Hour Act and the amount of paid holidays employers provide have both been important factors in shaping leisure during the period of industrialization. But the ideas that are promoted about leisure may be very complex and sometimes also contradictory. People may get conflicting messages. Local government has been an important provider of leisure services, from parks to swimming pools, which suggests that the state sees leisure as important to people; but from time to time central government ministers emphasize how much more important it is to do paid work than to enjoy leisure, views directed at the unemployed as well as the employed. The Sports Council for example, with state money, promotes sport as a way of people gaining enjoyment and physical fitness, but other motivations behind the promotion of sport may include fitter paid workers or mothers and keeping young unemployed youth off the streets. State schools teach physical education, often emphasizing its usefulness as preparation for leisure in adult life, but many school-children see P.E. as the antithesis of leisure. Similarly the same children may much dislike learning a foreign language, which is to be part of the National Curriculum in state schools, and which is seen as a preparation for paid work as much as for leisure, because they can't see any point in learning a language. Yet adults flock to adult education classes in physical activities like keep fit and languages as part of their leisure and are eager to spend their holidays in non-English-speaking countries. At the same time some of the leisure goods and services provided by the state industry and commerce cover an enormous variety and are perceived differently by different groups. Alcohol and tobacco are widely used for relaxation and leisure, but are seen as problematic for health by some groups. Bingo is seen as harmless fun by many players but as dangerous gambling by some religious groups. Local authority leisure centres are welcomed by many who want to swim, play five-a-side football or learn judo – but some politicians and ratepayers see leisure centres as a waste of money.

Sociologists are similarly divided in their views about leisure – whilst functionalists might stress the complementarity of work and leisure, and feminists the potentially liberating effects of leisure and sport, Marxists might point out that leisure is a means of controlling the population and of ensuring that they consume vast amounts of capitalist-produced goods and services and conflict theorists note how sport can exacerbate international tensions and how bureaucratic much leisure provision has become. Some think leisure is a good thing, others a bad thing; there are of course similar divisions between sociologists about the relationship between paid and unpaid work and unemployment and how all these things are changing. Some of these views will be considered in the final chapter.

Further reading

A book which surveys a considerable amount of research on leisure is K. Roberts' Leisure *(1980, Longman). Women's leisure is the subject of my own book* All Work and No Play: the Sociology of Women and Leisure *(1986, Open University Press). A useful although quite demanding collection of recent articles on sport and leisure is to be found in Horne, Jary, and Tomlinson's* Sport, Leisure and Social Relations *(1987, Routledge & Kegan Paul).*

6

Change: work, unemployment, and leisure

The question of change

So far we have considered formal employment, work carried on outside the formal economy (whether paid or unpaid), unemployment and patterns and experiences of leisure. In this final chapter I want to spend a little time looking at some of the wider issues raised by the earlier discussions of work and leisure. One of the most obvious questions raised by looking at the present and recent past is 'how are things changing and what will happen in the future?' Although it is an important question, it is also one which is difficult to answer. Predicting the future is not an easy task and even informed guesses can be totally wrong. In the 1880s some commentators thought compulsory education would produce better, more compliant employees and make industry more efficient and more able to compete with other countries in trade. But today people are still searching for ways of improving the links between industry and education and there are still complaints that schools don't produce good workers. In the 1930s when there was mass unemployment, many texts and books were written about how this shortage of work could usher in a new form of society where everyone had more leisure. Similar books have been written in the past decade. In the 1960s many were predicting that automation would totally change the future shape of paid work; but it did not. In the late 1980s people are saying that computerization will drastically alter both employment and leisure; it may or it may not. At the moment it is still too soon to tell.

Social and economic change is not a controlled rational thing which we or politicians or anyone else can set up and then sit back and watch happen. Of course some changes *are* planned, but they don't always turn out in the way expected. For example schemes set up by the Manpower Services Commission and other agencies to help the unemployed start their own businesses have resulted in a large number of women becoming their own boss; but women were not the target group at whom those schemes were aimed. The 1970 Equal Pay Act has not yet resulted in all women getting equal pay, nor have the Race Relations Acts eliminated racial prejudice in job interviews. Setting up leisure centres in most major towns and cities doesn't automatically change their populations from chain-smoking pub-goers into fit squash players who drink orange juice. Not all changes are planned anyway; no-one sat down in 1961 and said 'by 1984 more men will do more housework and more women will stay in jobs most of their adult lives', although certainly the women's movement and other political groups have contributed to this particular change, which has had a profound effect on patterns of work and leisure.

But we also have to be clear what we mean by the term change. It's very easy to say about work or leisure or the division of labour between men and women, 'Oh things are changing'. But a good sociology student will say, 'Wait a minute; what is changing, where is your evidence; over what time period is this change taking place; are you sure it isn't just a short term trend?' There is a real difference between short-term superficial change, say between the number of holidays taken in 1976 and the number taken in 1978, and long-term fundamental changes, like the shift from industrial manufacturing jobs into service industries in the job market, a process which has been going on for at least two decades, or the greater involvement of married women in employment since the 1960s, both of which have had profound effects on many aspects of our working lives, home life and leisure.

Activity

Go back to either the chapter on work in the formal economy (2), the one on unemployment (4) or the previous chapter to this, on leisure (5). Reread the chapter you've chosen. Try to find one of the books recommended for further reading. Skim through it, trying to get a broad picture of the evidence and arguments it presents. Then see if you can set out, firstly, any fundamental changes which are discussed (for example changes in legislation; major shifts in the economy; important alterations in leisure patterns or unemployment trends). Then set out changes which are only superficial, on present evidence.

Changes in formal employment

A huge number of changes have taken place in formal employment, many of them fairly significant for the kinds of jobs people do, where they do them, and what they do, but also many of them significant for people's life styles and leisure too. One of the most fundamental social and economic changes over the last three decades has been the changing pattern of women's employment, with more and more married women spending a much greater proportion of their lives in paid employment and taking shorter breaks in which

102

to have children. This has affected social relations at work, given rise to some new or expanding forms of work like childminding, has changed women's perception of their right to leisure, and has begun to shift the household division of labour. But of course there have been other agents of change operating here besides simply a greater requirement for female labour. These have included pressure from women themselves, in groups or individually, for greater independence, legislation on sex discrimination, changes in the ways girls are educated, easier divorce, and a decrease in the average family size.

Another fundamental change which has taken place is the shift from manufacturing industry to service employment. But you need to be aware here that although this affects the kind of work done (office or shop or hotel work rather than a car factory or shipbuilding) and where it is done (increasingly in the affluent South East of the UK rather than the north) it may not actually change the experience of work, the pay, the control exercised by employers over their employees, or the social relations of work. Similarly it may change our definitions of class but not necessarily end class divisions – a poorly paid office worker doing routine work still has a different position in the labour market and a different life style, as well as different life chances, when compared to a manager or a computer programmer. It does however mean that one can no longer assume that manual workers are working-class and non-manual workers are middle-class.

Another fundamental change has been the development of a much greater size of work organizations as monopolies and multi-national companies increase their grip, with the result that overall control is removed from the immediate work situation. So a managerial reaction to industrial action by employees may be to shut down the plant and move to another country. Size of organizations undoubtedly has an effect on the social relations of work too, with greater impersonality and possibly reduced employee morale.

The last three decades have also seen changes in the state's role in employment. These have included greater intervention in industrial disputes and employment legislation, but paradoxically the removal of minimum wage controls in a number of areas of employment. During the period between 1968 and 1979 the state's role as an employer increased considerably, but with the 1980s seeing many reductions in the level of public expenditure and with privatization of many nationalized concerns like British Telecom, British Gas, and British Petroleum, this may not be sustained. The state has also concerned itself with the training of young and adult workers in the period since the mid-1970s, a move which is linked to rising unemployment but which has also affected the ways in which young workers enter employment (increasingly for 16-year-olds through the Youth Training Scheme rather than directly into a job). There has also been concern, although this in itself is far from new, to encourage more job-related schooling, through schemes like the Technical and Vocational Educational Initiative and the Certificate of Pre-Vocational Education. It is intended that in 1988 a National Curriculum will be introduced into all schools, with a considerable science and technology component in it, which is perceived by the state as contributing towards a more skilled workforce, and industry is being encouraged to sponsor City Technology Colleges as alternatives to state secondary schools in urban areas.

There are of course all sorts of other changes taking place in formal employment, although many of them are still at the relatively superficial stage. These include computerization of jobs, which has undoubtedly affected the working conditions and autonomy of many workers (Crompton and Jones 1984) but which may or may not have more far-reaching effects on the distribution of work and leisure in our society. Other changes which are important but not yet at the fundamental stage are increases in part-time employment (especially significant for women), flexible hours of employment, where the overall number of hours stays the same but can be fitted into different time schedules of the individuals concerned;

job-sharing, where two people divide a single full-time job between them; contract working, which involves temporary employment, although often on a continuing basis; self-employment and homeworking of the kind which is well paid and involves jobs like computing.

Work in the informal economy

The difficulties of pointing to fundamental changes in this less well defined area are shown clearly in Chapter 3, where the theory that the hidden or formal economy grows as unemployment increases is shown not to hold up under the weight of empirical evidence (Pahl 1984). This in itself, of course, does not mean that the informal economy will not grow, but does suggest that it is not necessarily stimulated by unemployment. It is certainly apparent that unpaid work is receiving far more attention than it did until the 1970s, although it is not clear whether the apparent shifts in who does unpaid work in the home, as identified by Gershuny and Jones (1987), will be sustained. If it is and more men do take on a larger share of domestic responsibilities, then this could have considerable impact on women's lives (giving them greater opportunities for employment and leisure) and possibly changing the way men see paid work as well as altering forms of paid work (the latter might be necessary if more men took responsibility for childcare). But unpaid work does not just involve housework and childcare, but also care of the sick and people who are disabled and elderly. If, as in 1987 seems to be the case, the responsibilities of the state for disadvantaged groups is going to decrease, then this form of unpaid work may well increase. But things would have to go a lot further than they have at present before this could be viewed as a fundamental change.

Unemployment

It is relatively easy to identify the fundamental change in the area of unemployment: a massive increase in the numbers of people of employable age who are unable to find jobs, in the period since the mid-1970s up to the present day. But of course the impact of unemployment is unevenly felt: the young, the sick, the disabled, ethnic minorities, women, skilled manual workers, and those in the Northern areas of the UK have felt its brunt much more than middle-aged professionals living in the South-East of England. As the discussion in Chapter 4 showed, we cannot just assume that unemployment itself will bring about particular kinds of changes in people's life styles. Thus, time of itself does not always produce more leisure but often acute boredom and anxiety. If men are at home during the day rather than being out doing a job, it does not necessarily mean that they will do more than their previous meagre share of domestic work. Unemployment is not welcomed by most as a breathing space in which to rethink their futures. Its existence, despite many claims to the contrary, has not got rid of the work ethic; instead many unemployed people have been made to feel guilt because of the persistence of that ethic. As Bocock (1985) notes, the 'Real people have a paid job' idea is still firmly established in our society.

Leisure

The identification of fundamental changes in the area of leisure is made difficult by the problems associated with trying to split it off totally from other aspects of people's lives. Sometimes the same changes can affect work and leisure – women's increased employment, or computerization. But it is also difficult because there are still quite large gaps in our knowledge about leisure. Like the other phenomena we have considered, it is easier to see fundamental changes taking place over long periods of time, so that there is clearly a vast difference between a factory worker's experience of leisure in the mid-nineteenth century and the same worker's experience of leisure in the late twentieth century. But the differences may be less great than we suppose; certainly fewer hours of employment are involved and for many in full-time employment there is more paid holiday entitlement. But activities such as drinking are just as prevalent now as then, even though new leisure activities like TV, videos, and home computer games have appeared. One change which may be fundamental is the extent to which it is no longer only the leisure of employed males which is seen as important, but also women's leisure and that of children and the retired and the unemployed, although the change in actual experiences may lag behind. Leisure is also, as Clarke and Critcher (1985) point out, becoming increasingly consumption-dominated, revolving around a wide array of goods and services. It is also becoming something which is of growing interest to the state, in a variety of ways from the encouragement of fitness in the population because it can reduce medical costs if the population is healthier, to the targeting of particular groups like the young and the unemployed for the receipt of special schemes and concessions for leisure and sport participation. The concern of the state for leisure is often contradictory too – for central government receives a good deal of its revenue from tobacco and alcohol consumption, whilst giving money to the Sports Council to encourage more healthy life styles. Leisure itself is quite closely linked to certain aspects of the informal economy, including the communal economy. Brackenridge (1987) has pointed out how state schemes for extending leisure provision have begun to involve more and more voluntary groups, which sometimes gives rise to difficulties and problems in the schemes themselves.

Work, leisure, and the future

Some of the problems of talking about changes in work and leisure have been identified during this brief discussion. But, going on from this point, Clarke and Critcher (1985) suggest that there are yet further problems with the ways in which some sociologists analyse change:

107

- Quantitative changes (e.g. a drop in the average hours of employment worked) are often muddled up with qualitative changes (for example it is thought that because of fewer hours of employment, people will develop more satisfying life styles which are more oriented to leisure). You have already seen in the chapter on unemployment that an increase in the sheer number of hours without employment per week does not necessarily lead the unemployed into a new and satisfying life full of leisure.

- Potential consequences of change are often discussed as though they were inevitable consequences: that for example the introduction of micro-computers into employment 'automatically' brings about less routine jobs and hence a more leisured society, or that unemployment produces rethinking about life styles and a similarly more leisured society as well as a more equal division of labour in the home.

- Some discussions of change, particularly those which talk about the disappearance of the work ethic and its replacement by the leisure ethic, or about the vanishing of class boundaries, may, in their focus on one particular issue, miss out other important features of our society. For example office workers can end up with conditions and pay little different from those of factory workers, despite the apparent significance of the shift from manufacturing to service industries and even though in theory non-manual workers are supposed to be superior and more middle-class than manual workers. This theory has never worked well for women workers anyway, since they are usually just as disadvantaged in low-paid office jobs as they are in manual jobs like cleaning. However, it is worth pointing out that even if these changes don't end class divisions, they can still have important effects, for example on voting behaviour.

Clarke and Critcher's (1985) comments arise in the course of a discussion in their book about debates about post-industrial society theories and the shortcomings of these. The kinds of issues about work and leisure that have been considered in this book are often a prelude in the work of other writers (for example Roberts 1981, Parker 1983, Jenkins and Sherman 1981) to talking about future prospects for the development of society in general. Often this takes the form of arguing about whether in future people in society will do less work and enjoy more leisure (with work frequently being equated only with paid employment). Two particular stimuli to this 'will we have a leisure society?' argument at the present time are the developments in micro-electronics and computerization (which affects work *and* leisure) and the increases in mass unemployment. Clarke and Critcher outline these variants of debate about the future shape of society and although in this instance they are referring mainly to theorists writing about leisure, their categorization applies equally to those writing primarily about work.

- ## No real change

  Roberts (1981, 1983) sees no real prospects of radical changes taking place in the distribution of work and leisure and in the ways these are experienced and does not, despite his arguments about the preference of the young un-employed to remain outside the formal economy, see the work ethic disappearing and its replacement by a leisure society.

- ## Pessimism or scepticism about change

  This view does not say that no change is taking place, but is pessimistic or sceptical about the likely effects of that change on society. Clarke and Critcher suggest that Parker (1983), whilst acknowledging the impact of new technology on work and leisure patterns, takes a sceptical view of the effects of such changes. Parker does not foresee a massive replacement of workers by technology except where technology is cheaper than labour, and argues that new part-time, contract working in many service industries makes this less likely. Where unemployment does occur for this reason, the effects are likely to be negative – a destruction of work rather than the creation of new forms of leisure. In the field of leisure, Parker also does not see any particular changes affecting the mass of ordinary people coming about as new technology provides fresh means of entertainment in the home. No particular blurring of the line between work and leisure is thought likely to occur. Carrington and Leaman (1983), from a very different theoretical perspective, take a similarly sceptical view of attempts to use leisure to replace work for the young unemployed, contending that this will simply mean a widening division between the employed and unemployed, with the latter lacking both motivation and the money necessary for extensive leisure. Clarke and Critcher's own position can also be fitted in under this heading, since they suggest that the dynamics of capitalist society are such that there is no possibility of changes like the development of micro-electronic technology being used to benefit most of the population either in terms of work or leisure. Nor do they see class divisions disappearing.

- ● *Optimism*

Under this heading Clarke and Critcher place those writers like the Rapoports (1975) whose discussion of the place and changing role of leisure in the family cycle leads them to claim that developments like shorter and more flexible forms of paid work may lead to new life styles and better use of leisure resources. Leisure planning and counselling is advocated to enable people to get more out of their leisure time. A similarly optimistic view, although from a rather different political perspective, is taken by Jenkins and Sherman (1981) who discuss the opportunities afforded by a shortage of paid employment and new technology to restructure society and our life styles so that the available

110

jobs are shared around and everyone can enjoy more constructive leisure, rather than just a minority who might otherwise manage to hold on to conventional jobs. Whatever the strengths and weaknesses of their particular approach, Jenkins and Sherman do have the advantage of pointing out that different forms of society don't come about simply through a variety of changes to work and leisure or through technological and economic shifts; politics do enter into it quite strongly, not just at the level of the state but involving other groups too.

Activity

1 Try to set out the arguments for and against the view that current changes in work and leisure would be likely to lead to a society in which there was much more leisure for everyone. You may find it helpful to look at a book like Jenkins and Sherman (1981), Clarke and Critcher (1985), Veal (1987), or Parker (1983), so that you can see how particular writers construct their arguments.

2 What do you think a leisure society would look like? What, if any, role would paid and unpaid work have in such a society? How would a leisure society be organized? Would there still be a role for the state as well as private organizations? What would happen to divisions based on class, gender, and race; would they disappear altogether? Would it be necessary to educate people for leisure?

Conclusion

I hope this short book has not only given you some indication of the ways in which sociologists have explored the issues of work and leisure, but has also shown you how deeply central to our lives leisure and working are. In particular you should by now have realized how restricted are the conventional notions about what constitutes work and leisure and how much more those two things actually encompass. The theories and research which we have considered in this book are important if we are to develop systematic ideas and knowledge about the social world. But work and leisure are two areas where your own experiences can be extremely valuable, provided that you don't use these as a substitute for more detailed and more generalizable evidence, and some of the activities have been designed to help you make use of your own, your friends', and your family's experiences in this way. I have only been able to touch briefly on many issues here and have missed out others altogether, but the further reading should help those who have become interested by the study of leisure and work to delve more deeply. A lot of questions about work and leisure have been posed by researchers; many haven't been satisfactorily answered and may not be answerable by social scientists. But a great many of those questions aren't just abstract ones; they are part of the way in which our society and others will develop. Your own future work and leisure will be part of that development, long after you have forgotten this book and the course you were taking when you read it.

_____

Further reading

Jenkins and Sherman's (1981) The Leisure Shock *is a thought-provoking book, even if you don't agree with their argument, and covers what is happening to work and leisure now as well as in the future. Clarke and Critcher's (1985)* The Devil Makes Work: Leisure in Capitalist Britain *is much more demanding to read but worthwhile for its wide coverage; unlike Jenkins and Sherman the authors are aware of gender and race divisions as well as class ones. An interesting book which mainly focuses on work is C. Handy's (1985)* The Future of Work *(Blackwell), which has the advantage of engaging with some of the issues about the informal economy.*

A traditional approach to the future of leisure is taken by Veal (1987) in Leisure and the Future *(Allen & Unwin) but there are some interesting chapters on different perspectives and a readable chapter on leisure forecasting.*

References

Abbot, P. and Sapsford, R. (1987) *Women and Social Class*, London: Tavistock.

Alden, J. (1981) 'Holding two jobs; an examination of "moonlighting"', in S. Henry (ed.) *Can I Have It In Cash?*, London: Astragal Books.

Berger, P. (1963) *Invitation to Sociology*, Harmondsworth: Penguin.

Berger, P. (1964) *The Human Shape of Work*, New York: Macmillan.

Blackburn, R. and Mann, M. (1979) *The Working Class in the Labour Market*, London: Macmillan.

Bocock, R. (1985) 'Ideologies of work', Unit 15, Open University Course DE325 *Work and Society*, Milton Keynes: Open University Press.

Brackenridge, C. (1987) 'Women and community recreation in the UK', unpublished paper.

Braham, P. and Rhodes, E. (1981) 'Ethnic minorities and the labour market', Unit 11, E354 *Ethnic Minorities and Community Relations*, Milton Keynes: Open University Press.

Braham, P., Rhodes, E., and Pearn, M. (1981) *Discrimination and*

Disadvantage in Employment, London: Harper & Row.

Braverman, H. (1974) *Labor and Monopoly Capital*, New York: Monthly Review Press.

Britten, N. and Heath, A. (1983) 'Women, men and social class', in E. Garmarnikov, J. Purvis, D. Morgan, and D. Taylorson (eds) *Gender, Class and Work*, London: Heinemann.

Burgoyne, J. (1985) 'Unemployment and married life', *Unemployment Unit Bulletin* 18: 7–10.

Burns, T. (1973) 'Leisure in industrial society', in M. Smith, S. Parker, and C. Smith (eds) *Leisure and Society in Britain*, London: Allen Lane, the Penguin Press.

Carrington, B. and Leaman, O. (1983) 'Work for some and sport for all', *Youth and Policy*, 1, 3: 10–15.

Clarke, J. and Critcher, C. (1985) *The Devil Makes Work: Leisure in Capitalist Britain*, London: Macmillan.

Clarke, J., Critcher, C., and Johnson, R. (1979) *Working Class Culture*, London: Hutchinson.

Cockburn, C. (1983) *Brothers: Male Dominance and Technological Change*, London: Pluto Books.

Coyle, A. (1984) *Redundant Women*, London: Women's Press.

Cragg, A. and Dawson, T. (1981) 'Qualitative research amongst homeworkers', Department of Employment Research Paper 21, London: HMSO.

Crompton, R. and Jones, G. (1984) *White Collar Proletariat: Deskilling and Gender in Clerical Work*, London: Macmillan.

Crompton, R., Jones, G., and Reid, S. (1982) 'Contemporary clerical work: a case study of local government' in J. West (ed.) *Women, Work and the Labour Market*, London: Routledge & Kegan Paul.

Davidoff, L. (1976) 'Landscape with figures: home and community in English society', in J. Mitchell and A. Oakley (eds) *The Rights and Wrongs of Women*, Harmondsworth: Penguin.

Deem, R. (1986) *All Work and No Play: the Sociology of Women and Leisure*, Milton Keynes: Open University Press.

Deem, R. and Salaman, G. (1985) (eds) *Work, Culture and Society*, Milton Keynes: Open University Press.

Delphy, C. (1984) *Close to Home*, London: Hutchinson.

Dex, S. (1985) *The Sexual Division of Work*, Brighton: Harvester Press.

Ditton, J. (1974) 'The fiddling salesman: connivance at corruption', *New Society*, Nov. 28th, 1974.

115

Dixey, R. and Talbot, M. (1982) *Women, Leisure and Bingo*, Leeds: Trinity and All Saints College.

Dumazdier, J. (1974) *Sociology of Leisure*, Amsterdam: Elsevier.

Dunning, E. and Sheard, K. (1969) *Barbarians, Gentlemen, and Players*, Oxford: Martin Robertson.

Edgell, S. (1980) *Middle Class Couples*, London: Allen & Unwin.

Elias, N. and Dunning, E. (1969) 'The quest for excitement in leisure', *Society and Leisure*, 2: 50–58.

Finnegan, R. (1985a) 'What is work?' Unit 1, Open University Course DE325 *Work and Society*, Milton Keynes: Open University Press.

Finnegan, R. (1985b) 'Working outside formal employment', in R. Deem and G. Salaman (eds) *Work, Culture and Society*, Milton Keynes: Open University Press.

Freedman, M. (1985) 'The search for shelters', in K. Thompson (ed.) *Work, Employment and Society*, Milton Keynes: Open University Press.

Gail, S. (1985) 'The housewife', in C. Littler (ed.) *The Experience of Work*, Aldershot: Gower/Heinemann.

Gershuny, J. and Jones, S. (1987) 'The changing work/leisure balance in Britain: 1961–1984', in J. Horne, D. Jary, and A. Tomlinson (eds) *Sport, Leisure and Social Relations*, Sociological Review Monograph 33, London: Routledge & Kegan Paul.

Gershuny, J. and Pahl, R. (1985) 'Britain in the decade of the three economies', in C. Littler (ed.) *The Experience of Work*, Aldershot: Gower/Heinemann.

Glyptis, S. and Chambers, D. (1982) 'No place like home', *Leisure Studies*, 1: 247–62.

Goldthorpe, J., Lockwood, D., Bechofer, F., and Platt, J. (1969) *The Affluent Worker in the Class Structure*, Cambridge: Cambridge University Press.

Green, E., Hebron, S., and Woodward, D. (1987) *Leisure and Gender: A Study of Sheffield Women's Leisure Experiences*, London: Sports Council/ESRC.

Griffin, C. (1985) *Typical Girls*, London: Routledge & Kegan Paul.

Hakim, C. (1984a) 'Homework and outwork – national estimates from two surveys', *Employment Gazette*, 92, 1: 7–12.

Hakim, C. (1984b) 'Employers' use of homework, outwork and freelances', *Employment Gazette*, 92, 4: 144–50.

Hall, C. (1982) 'The butcher, the baker, the candlestick maker: the

116

shop and the family in the Industrial Revolution', in F. Whitelegg
et al, (eds) *The Changing Experience of Women*, Oxford: Martin
Robertson.

Haralambros, M. (1985) (2nd Edn) *Sociology: themes and perspectives*, London: Bell & Hyman.

Hatch, S. (1980) *Outside the State: Voluntary Organisations in
Three English Towns*, London: Croom Helm.

Horne, J., Jary, D., and Tomlinson, A. (1987) (eds) *Sport, Leisure
and Social Relations*, Sociological Review Monograph 33,
London: Routledge & Kegan Paul.

Jenkins, C. and Sherman, B. (1981) *The Leisure Shock*, London:
Eyre Methuen.

Karn, V. (1977) *Retiring to the Seaside*, London: Routledge &
Kegan Paul.

McKee, L. and Bell, C. (1984) 'His unemployment; her problem. The
domestic and marital consequences of male unemployment',
unpublished paper given to 1984 British Sociological Association
Conference.

McNeill, P. (1985) *Research Methods*, London: Tavistock.

Malos, E. (1980) *The Politics of Housework*, London: Allison &
Busby.

Mars, G. (1985) 'Hotel pilferage: a case study in occupational theft',
in C. Littler (ed.) *The Experience of Work*, Aldershot: Gower /
Heinemann.

Marsden, D. (1982) *Workless*, London: Croom Helm.

Martin, C. and Roberts, J. (1984) *Women and Employment: a
Lifetime Perspective*, London: HMSO, Department of Employment.

Martin, R. and Wallace, J. (1984) *Working Women in Recession*,
Oxford: Oxford University Press.

Maynard, M. (1985) 'Houseworkers and their work', in R. Deem
and G. Salaman (eds) *Work, Culture and Society*, Milton Keynes:
Open University Press.

Oakley, A. (1974) *Housework*, Oxford: Martin Robertson.

Oakley, A. (1976) *Housewife*, Harmondsworth: Penguin.

Pahl, R. (1984) *Divisions of Labour*, Oxford: Blackwell.

Parker, S. (1983) *Leisure and Work*, London: Allen & Unwin.

Pollert, A. (1981) *Girls, Wives; Factory Lives*, London: Macmillan.

Rapoport, R. and R.N. (1975) *Leisure and the Family Life Cycle*,
London: Routledge & Kegan Paul.

Roberts, K. (1981) *Leisure*, London: Longman.

— (1983) *Youth and Leisure*, London: Allen & Unwin.

Roberts, K., Duggan, J., and Noble, M. (1981) 'Unregistered youth unemployment', Department of Employment Research Paper 31, London: HMSO.

Salaman, G. (1985) Review 2, Unit 12, Open University Course DE325, *Work and Society*, Milton Keynes: Open University Press.

— (1986) *Working*, Chichester: Ellis Horwood.

Scraton, S. (1987) 'Boys muscle in where angels fear to tread: girls' subcultures and physical activities', in J. Horne, D. Jary, and A. Tomlinson, (eds) *Sport, Leisure and Social Relations*, Sociological Review Monograph 33, London: Routledge & Kegan Paul.

Seabrook, J. (1983) *Unemployment*, London: Paladin Books.

Sharpe, S. (1984) *Double Identity*, London: Penguin.

Sinfield, A. (1981) *What Unemployment Means*, Oxford: Martin Robertson.

Slattery, M. (1986) *Official Statistics*, London: Tavistock.

Smith, D. (1981) 'Discrimination against applicants for white collar jobs', in P. Braham, E. Rhodes, and M. Pearn, *Discrimination and Disadvantage in Employment*, London: Harper & Row.

Smith, J. (1987) 'Men and Women at Play: gender, life cycle and leisure', in D. Jary, J. Horne, and A. Tomlinson (eds) *Sport, Leisure and Social Relations*, London and Keele: Routledge & Kegan Paul.

Social Trends 1985 (1985), London: HMSO.

Social Trends 1986 (1986), London: HMSO.

Social Trends 1987 (1987), London: HMSO.

Szalai, A. (1972) *The Use of Time*, The Hague: Mouton.

Taylor, F.W. (reprinted 1964) *Scientific Management*, London: Harper & Row.

Terkel, S. (1983) (2nd Edn) *Working*, Harmondsworth: Penguin.

Thompson, E.P. (1967) 'Time, work-discipline and industrial capitalism', *Past and Present*, 38, December.

Thompson, J. (1983) *Learning Liberation*, London: Croom Helm.

Tomlinson, A. (1979) *Leisure and the role of voluntary clubs and groups*, London: SSRC/Sports Council.

Troyna, B. and Smith, D. (1983) *Racism, School and the Labour Market*, Leicester: National Youth Bureau Studies in Research Series.

118

Tysoe, M. (1985) 'Tourism is good for you', *New Society*, 16 August: 228–30.

Wallace, C. (1986) 'From girls and boys to women and men: the social reproduction of gender roles in the transition from school to (un)employment', in S. Walker and L. Barton (eds) *Youth, Unemployment and Schooling*, Milton Keynes: Open University Press.

Weiss, L. (1987) 'Youth in a deindustrializing economy', paper given to Westhill Sociology of Education Conference.

West, J. (1982) (ed.) *Women, Work and the Labour Market*, London: Routledge & Kegan Paul.

Wilensky, H.L. (1960) 'Work, careers and social integration', *International Social Science Journal*, 4: 543–60.

Willis, P. (1977) *Learning to Labour*, Farnborough: Saxon House.

Wrench, J. and Lee, G. (1983) 'A subtle hammering – young black people and the labour market', in B. Troyna and D. Smith, *Racism, School and the Labour Market*, Leicester: National Youth Bureau Studies in Research Series.

Yeandle, S. (1984) *Women's Working Lives*, London: Tavistock.

Index

121